D0549543

Just

For class or
self-study

Reading and Writing

Jeremy Harmer
& Carol Lethaby

 Marshall Cavendish
Education

Photo acknowledgements

p.11 a, ©Arkansas Democrat-Gazette, b, ©Rene Burri/Magnum Photos, c, ©Associated Press, AP, d, ©Corbis; p.12, ©Will Counts, used with kind permission of Mrs V. Counts; p.15, ©Doninic Burke/Alamy; p.17, ©Royalty Free/Corbis; p.18, ©Royalty Free/Corbis, p.22, ©Tom Jenkins; p.23, ©PA Photos/EPA, p.24, ©Sami Sarkis/Sarkis Images/Alamy; p.25, ©Tony Kyriacou/Rex Features; p.26 background, ©John Lawreence Photography/Alamy, insert, ©NANO CALVO/VWPICS/Visual&Written SL/Alamy; p.28, ©Anthony Redpath/Corbis; p.34 top, Comstock Images/Alamy, middle, Bananastock/Alamy, bottom, ©Comstock Images/Alamy; p.42 left, ©Royalty Free/Corbis, top centre, ©Joe Sohm/Alamy, bottom centre, ©Michael Saul/Brand X Pictures/Alamy, right, ©Michael Saul/Brand X Pictures/Alamy; p.45, ©Shout/Alamy; p.47 top right, ©Herbie Knott/Rex Features, bottom, ©SuperStock/Alamy; p.52, Comstock Images/Alamy; p.55, Dr Arthur Agatson, ©Wilfredo Lee/Associated Press, Dr Robert Atkins, ©Associated Press, Atkins Centre, Dr Barry Sears, ©Bobbie Bush, used with kind permission of HarperCollins, USA, Bernice Weston, ©Joe Partridge/Rex Features; p.61 top-bottom, ©Gregory Pace/Corbis, ©Gregory Pace/Corbis, ©Cinema Photo/Corbis, ©Photo Japan/Alamy; p.63, ©Keith Morris; p.70, ©SIPA Press/Rex Features; p.72 both, ©TM & copyright 20th Century Fox/Rex Features; p.82, ©Kevin Lock/ZUMA/Corbis; p.83, ©Reuters/Corbis; p.84, ©Sam Barcroft (SFT) Rex Features; p.87, ©Random House used with kind permission; p.92 all, ©Buenavist/Everett/Rex; p.93, ©Patrick Combs, courtesy of Good Thinking Company; p.95 all, ©Rex Features; p.99 left, ©Brooks Craft/Corbis, centre, ©Paul Taylor, right, ©David Sillitoe

Marshall Cavendish ELT
119 Wardour Street
London W1F 0UW

Designed by Hart McLeod, Cambridge
Editorial development by Ocelot Publishing, Oxford, with Geneviève Talon
Illustrations by Yane Christiansen

Printed and bound by EDELVIVES, Spain

Text acknowledgements

p.8 Dream or Nightmare, based upon articles by Dan Kennedy and Mark Meltzer; p.8 Attitudes to Money based upon an article by Suze Orman; p.18 How could we get it so wrong, based upon an article by Jonathan Glancy, ©Guardian Newspapers Limited; p.19 Surprise, based upon an article by Kathryn Flett, ©Guardian Newspapers Limited 1997; p.22-23 Based upon an article from Observer Sport Monthly, by Tim Adams and Ed Douglas; p.24 Trainspotting based upon an article by Mark Oliver; 28-30 The Anger Page, based upon various articles; p.32 Smiling and Frowning based upon an article from www.straightdope.com; p. 37 Based on various articles mainly from the Flying Doctor, by John Gibb; p.39-40 Finding out about the Future, based upon various website articles; p.45 Article 1, by Sarah Wilkin, ©Adhoc Publishing; p.45 Article 2 based upon an article by Max Luscher; p.45 Article 3 by Victoria Moore, ©The Independent on Sunday 6.05.01; p.45 Article 4 based upon an article from the Observer; p. 47 Edward De Bono reproduced kindly by www.sixhats.com/edbio.htm; p.48 Article based upon Six Thinking Hats by Sylvie Labelle; p.53 Article 1 granted by kind permission of the Vegan Action Group; p.53 Article 2 granted by kind permission of the Greenpeace Organisation; p.53 Article 3 granted by kind permission of Dr Mercola; p.53 Article 4 based upon an article by Monsanto; p.56 Articles based upon information from various websites; p.59 Statistical Table based upon information from the Vegan Research Panel; p.59 Pie Chart based upon information from Balwynhs School, Australia; p.61 The New Blonde Bombshell, by Brian Bates, ©Brian Bates; p.63-65 Radio 2 website by Mick Fitzsimmons, reproduced kindly by BBC Radio 2; p70 Notes by Elenor Coppola published by Simon and Schuster, © Faber and Faber; p.73 Climate Change more Dangerous than Terrorism, based upon an article by William S Kowinski; p.74 Adrian Mole The Wilderness Years by Sue Townsend, ©Sue Townsend 1993.Permission Granted by The Curtis Brown Group; p.80 Radio Times article, reproduced kindly by The Radio Times; p.84 About a Boy, by Nick Hornby, © Penguin Group USA; p.86 Paula by Isabel Allende, ©HarperCollins; p.86 The Green Mile, by Stephen King ©Stephen King; p.89 The Curious Incident of the Dog in the Night Time, by Mark Haddon.Used by permission of the Random House Group; p.92 When a Crime is not a Crime? Based upon an article by L.D Meagher; p.93 Man 1 Bank 0, based upon an article by Lisa Margonelli; p.95 Coughing for a Million, an article based upon various websites; p.99 Midsummer, Tobago from Sea Grapes by Derek Walcott, published by Jonathan Cape. Used by permission of the Random House Group; p.99 Like a Beacon by Grace Nichols, ©Grace Nichols. Permission granted by Curtis Brown Group Ltd; p.99 Handbag by Ruth Fainlight, ©Ruth Fainlight; p.101 Why Cat and Dog are no Longer Friends based upon a old Indian Folk Tale by Philip Sherlock

Contents

Skills titles available at intermediate level

Just Reading and Writing 0-462-00711-1

Just Grammar 0-462-00713-8

Just Listening and Speaking 0-462-00714-6 (with Audio CD)

Just Vocabulary 0-462-00712-X (with Audio CD)

Introduction

For the student

Just Reading and Writing (*Upper Intermediate*) is one of two skills books designed for you to study on your own, or together with other students and a teacher. It will help you improve your reading and writing skills in English.

We have chosen the texts and tasks carefully to offer an interesting and challenging mix of topics and language styles. We have included contemporary uses of English such as email and the Internet.

This book has a lot of practice exercises to help you with reading and writing. When you see this symbol ( ) at the end of an exercise it means that you can refer to the answer key at the back of the book and check your answers there.

Although we encourage the use of dictionaries, our advice is not to use one until you have done all the exercises in a section. If you use your dictionary too early you may find it more difficult to understand the general meaning of the text.

We are confident that this book will help you progress in English and, above all, that you will enjoy using it.

For the teacher

The *Just* skills books at the Upper Intermediate level can be used on their own or in combination, or as supplementary material to support other materials. They have been written and designed using a consistent methodological approach that allows them to be used easily together. They are designed in such a way that they can be used either in class or by the students working on their own.

Just Reading and Writing consists of 14 units containing a variety of reading texts and activities on subjects such as money, photography, anger, diets, poems, appearance and hobbies of all kinds. These are designed to give students experience of reading and writing in different styles and genres of English. There's a comprehensive answer key at the back of the book.

Our aim has been to provide texts and tasks that are themselves stimulating and that could lead to any number of student activities once the exercises in this book have been completed.

We are confident that you will find this book a real asset and that you will also want to try the other title at the Upper Intermediate level, *Just Listening and Speaking*.

A Lottery dreams

1 Read this article, *Dream or nightmare?*, quickly. Where do sentences *a–g* fit in the article? The first one is done for you.

a Lynette Nichols was a bookkeeper before she won about $17 million in the lottery. ...**3**...

b So why does a sudden win cause so many problems? ....

c Brett Peterson was just 19 and working as a busboy in a small restaurant in California. ....

d So, do you still want to win the lottery? ....

e On top of this, big winners are not prepared for the new expectations that people now have of them. ....

f For many, a big win in the lottery is their dream ....

g John and Sandy from Ohio won about $12 million and almost immediately the letters and phone calls started. ....

DREAM OR NIGHTMARE?

Have you always dreamed of winning the lottery? Everyone does, don't they?

After reading Janet Bloom's article, you might change your mind.

.... and so they buy tickets every week hoping for a dream come true. People think that when they win they will be able to stop doing their boring job and live a life of luxury. But if their numbers really do come up, that dream often becomes a nightmare.

.... When he found out he was going to receive a $2 million payout in the lottery, he immediately gave up work, lent money to all his friends, whether or not they would be able to pay it back, and went out on a wild spending spree. Within months he had huge credit card debts and no money left to pay them. A year later, he had taken a job as a sales clerk to try to make ends meet.

.... Did it bring her happiness? Not exactly. She and her husband immediately started fighting over money. She couldn't believe that he was wasting money on electronic toys for himself, while he objected to her buying expensive cars for her family. They ended up in court in a trial that cost them both hundreds of thousands of dollars and, of course, they're now divorced.

.... Everyone, from crazy inventors to people needing help putting their kids through college, wanted a donation from them. Their own kids lost all their friends when they moved house to a more expensive neighborhood and they spent way too much time and energy worrying about their own safety. And to make matters worse, they both lost their jobs as accountants.

.... Well, it seems that a large win can put enormous stress on people who are not prepared for it. The majority of people who win are people who did not have a lot of money before. They tend to come from blue-collar backgrounds and have been used to working full time and living 'pay-check to pay-check'. When they get this unexpected windfall, they don't know how to cope. Very often they stop working and they move house. But these are probably the two worst things they can do. Who lives in wealthy neighborhoods? Wealthy people of course – people who are used to having and spending money. Moving to these areas alienates lottery winners from their familiar world and friends. From one day to the next, they lose the structure that the working day offers and they no longer have the support system of neighbors who come from similar backgrounds around them. They find themselves surrounded by strangers from a different world with different life experiences, and on top of that, they have plenty of free time on their hands.

.... .Their friends expect them to be generous and pay for everything and they receive requests from strangers asking them to donate money to a particular cause. Very often, lottery winners do not have much experience in investing money wisely and end up making disastrous financial decisions, which quickly eat up their winnings. Many past lottery winners have commented on how easy it is to spend a lot of money very quickly once they started to believe, on a daily basis, that 'money is no object'.

.... .If you do win, the best advice is probably to get yourself some good, independent financial advice and, more importantly, to be aware that becoming rich overnight could radically change your life – and not necessarily for the better.

We want to hear from **YOU**.
How do you handle money?
What would you do if you won the lottery?
Would you save or spend? Write and let us know.

2   Read the article again. Complete the table with information from the text about Brett, Lynette, and John and Sandy. The first one is done for you.

	Brett	Lynette	John and Sandy
Job(s)	a _busboy_ b	f	j ....
How much did they win?	c	g	k ....
Main problems	d .... e	h .... i	l .... m .... n ....

3   Explain the meaning of the following words as they appear in the text.

a objected to (paragraph 3) ....

b windfall (paragraph 5) ....

c alienates (paragraph 5) ....

d wisely (paragraph 6) ....

e disastrous (paragraph 6) ....

f eat up (paragraph 6) ....

g overnight (paragraph 7) ....

Language in chunks

4   Look at how these phrases are used in the text and then use them in the sentences which follow. You may have to change them slightly to make them fit.

a dream come true   to end up (doing something)   (to have) time on one's hands
to make matters worse   money is no object   way too much (something)

a That girl is never at school and when she has .... she gets into trouble.

b They spent all their money and .... they then borrowed money to buy a car.

c The cost of the project doesn't matter at all. ....

d We didn't know what to buy with the money we won and we .... depositing it all in a bank account that gives high interest.

e Kevin had .... money as a kid – his parents gave him everything he wanted – and now he doesn't know how to manage his own financial affairs.

f Getting this new job was .... for me. I really enjoy it, the hours are great and the pay is good.

B Attitudes to money

1 **Look up these expressions in a dictionary and write your own definition for each one.**

a penny-pincher ....

b spendthrift ....

c on the right track ....

d daredevil ....

What's your attitude to money? Are you a penny-pincher, a spendthrift, a daredevil, or on the right track? Take this quiz and find out.

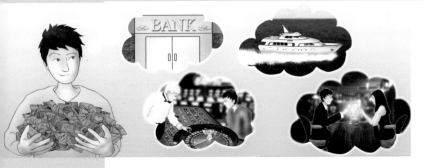

Circle the letter corresponding to the answer which best applies to you.

1 Saving

A When you receive a gift of money, you don't even consider saving it. Instead, you buy something extravagant.

B Every month you save as much money as you can, even when it means doing without 'luxuries' such as some new clothes, a new CD or a movie.

C You have no money in savings, you owe people money and you have no savings account.

D You save a manageable amount of money every month, and you have specific ideas about what you are going to do with it.

2 Spending

A You buy what you want, when you want it – on credit if necessary – because you just know that you'll earn the money to pay for it.

B You often put off buying the essential things you need, although you can easily afford to buy them.

C Shopping is a competitive sport for you. If a friend buys the latest watch, jacket or trainers, you have to have them, too. Your wardrobe is full of clothes you've hardly ever worn.

D You buy what you need, you aren't often tempted by what you don't need, and most importantly you understand the difference between 'need' and 'want'.

3 Bills and records

A You can't be bothered to look at records of what you spend and don't spend. Shouldn't the banks keep track of your money?

B You check all your account statements frequently, either by phone or online, to make sure your records match exactly. You keep your cash point receipts, credit card vouchers and cancelled cheques for years.

C Because you don't pay your bills on time, you often owe a late fee, and sometimes you can't even find your bills amid the clutter on your desk. You pay the minimum amount due on your credit cards.

D Your accounts are balanced and your bills are paid as soon as they come in.

4 Giving

A When it comes to giving things to people, you tend to be impulsive and you're likely to give more than you can afford.

B You give things to people but you give relatively small amounts compared to what you can afford to give.

C You repeatedly give away large amounts of money, especially for social events and raffles, even though you don't have any savings.

D Every month, you donate the same affordable amount to the causes of your choice. You've carefully budgeted your money and your time to support the causes that are important to you.

Count how many of each letter you have circled and record the number below. The biggest number will reveal your attitude to money.

A ....   B ....   C ....   D ....

2 Now look at *Interpreting the results* at the bottom of this page. What kind of attitude to money do you have, according to the quiz?

....

3 Read these pieces of advice and match them to the descriptions of the different money personalities.

a You have to start spending money to make money. Why deprive yourself of fun and friends? Learn to enjoy money more.

....

b Continue to budget carefully and set yourself clear financial goals. This is the best way to deal with money.

....

c If you think about the things that are really important to you, you'll find that they are not the things you bought, but the things that money can't buy. You need to be honest with yourself and who you are. Ask your friends and family to help you.

....

d You're in a dangerous situation and now is the time to stop and think about the future. You need to think about who you are and what you want in life, and start to save money.

....

4 Match the meanings with the words from the text in blue.

a little lottery
b attracted to (even though you know you shouldn't)
c don't want to because you haven't got the energy
d financial records
e in the middle of the mess
f place where you keep clothes
g look carefully so you can remember the details
h unnecessarily expensive
i that you can afford

5 Now use the correct word from Activity 4 to complete these sentences.

a After she read the .... from the bank, she realised that she would have to start saving more money.
b John .... get cash from the machine so he always uses his credit card.
c She went to the .... , took out her new dress and slipped it over her head. It had been worth every penny!
d The designer shoes were .... and she couldn't afford them, so she left the store without even trying them on.
e She couldn't find her Discman .... in her bedroom.
f He bought a couple of tickets for the .... , hoping that he would win a prize for his family.
g I know you don't earn much money, but at least your flat is small and the rent is ....
h Why did he find it so hard to .... what he was spending? Maybe he should start writing it all down.
i She was .... the little black dress, but it was really too expensive.

Interpreting the results

A DAREDEVIL
You are generous, true, but you are too often reckless. You identify yourself more by what you do with money than by who you are, which means that somewhere along the way you've lost a sense of your own identity.

B PENNY-PINCHER
You are a penny-pincher. You have more than enough money, but you won't spend your money. You are afraid of never having enough.

C SPENDTHRIFT
Your spending is way out of control. Sooner, rather than later, financial reality will catch up with you – with huge credit card interest or, in the worst case, bankruptcy. Wouldn't you rather put a stop to it before that happens?

D ON THE RIGHT TRACK
Congratulations! You are creating a life where people come first, then money, then things. You have learned to value who you are over what you have. You are on the right road.

··C Mind maps

1 Mind maps can be used to help you to brainstorm and organise your ideas before you start a piece of writing.

Look at this mind map. Which one do you think is the central theme, *a*, *b* or *c*?

a winning the lottery
b seeing a financial advisor
c investing for the future

alienation
Don't know how to invest
Invest for the future
Give things to family and friends
Problems
....
....
Possible things to do with money
People ask for money
stress
Spend it on material things
Make donations

2 Complete the mind map here with your own ideas and associations.

What is my attitude to money?
save?
What will I do if I win the lottery?
spend?

3 Look at the end of the article from page 7.

We want to hear from **YOU**.
How do you handle money?
What would you do if you won the lottery?
Would you save or spend? Write and let us know.

Write a short letter in answer to the article. Divide your writing into three paragraphs and use your mind map to help you.

Paragraph 1:
my attitude to money

Paragraph 2:
why I would spend some money and what I would spend it on

Paragraph 3:
why I would save some money and how I would save it

EXAMPLE:
My name is Yong Min and I am a student at the University of Taegu. I am a very careful person with money. If I have any extra money I always save it, because I might need it one day.

If I won the lottery, I would spend some of the money and save some of it. I would spend some money on ...

4 Look at the mind map that you created. Have you included all the important ideas in your piece of writing?

UNIT 2

●●A More than a moment

1 Look at the photographs and read the text on page 12. Which photograph illustrates the text?

2 Read the following sentences and then decide where they should go in the text on page 12. There is one sentence too many. The first one is done for you.

a And because of this black children were finally admitted to whites-only schools. ....
b The first test case of this ruling occurred in Little Rock, Arkansas, in 1957 when nine black students tried to attend classes at the Central High School. ...**1**....
c Finally, at the ceremony 40 years later, she and her victim met face to face. ....
d He called for greater understanding between races, a call which echoes down the years in the wake of misunderstandings between different peoples and religions of the world. ....
e The photographs Counts took that day were soon published all over America and the world. ....
f William Counts had been a student at the Central High School himself. ....
g And so there was. ....

MORE THAN A MOMENT

Some photographs, like the one taken by photographer William Counts outside the Central High School in Little Rock, Arkansas (USA) all those years ago, are so powerful that they help to change the course of history.

In 1954 the Supreme Court of the United States of America decided that <u>segregated</u> <u>education</u> (previously accepted as 'separate but equal') was unconstitutional.

1 [ ] But racism was a fact of life in those days, and many white Americans were bitterly opposed to multiracial schooling. The governor of the state of Arkansas, Orval Faubus, sent soldiers of the National Guard to the high school to stop black children from attending classes there, and to 'maintain order'.

2 [ ] Now 26 years old, he arrived at the scene with his camera after only a few days as a photographer with the *Arkansas Democrat* newspaper. Nobody paid him too much attention because he was a local man. As a result he was not attacked by the angry crowds as many photographers from out of town were that day, and he was able to take his famous picture.

Counts had recognised immediately that the moment the black students tried to get to the school there would be trouble. 3 [ ] Elizabeth Eckford, the first of the nine, was turned back by the soldiers, and Counts, running backwards in front of her, started taking his pictures. And that was how the world saw a picture of a 15-year-old white girl, Hazel Bryan, shouting abuse at the black student. 'The crowd were right in her ear,' Counts recalled many years later, 'they were yelling their hate, but she [Eckford] never lost her composure, she just remained so dignified, so determined in what she was doing.'

4 [ ] They caused outrage. Dwight D. Eisenhower, the president of the United States, saying how moved he was by pictures of the 'disgraceful occurrences', took control of the National Guard and ordered federal troops to escort the 'Little Rock Nine' to school despite the objections of the Arkansas governor. Desegregated education had begun.

Forty years later, the nine black students were awarded the congressional medal of honour by American president Bill Clinton in a ceremony at the Central High School. In his speech, he said, 'Like so many Americans, I can never fully repay my debt to these nine people. For with their innocence, they purchased more freedom for me, too, and for all white people.' But he was far from optimistic about the future of race relations: 'Today, children of every race walk through the same door, but then they often walk down different halls,' he said. 'Not only in this school, but across America, they sit in different classrooms, they eat at different tables. They even sit in different parts of the bleachers at the football game. Far too many communities are all white, all black, all Latino, all Asian. Indeed, too many Americans of all races have actually begun to give up on the idea of integration and the search for common ground.' 5 [ ]

And what of Hazel Bryan Massery, the girl with her face screwed up in anger and hatred? Five years after the photograph was taken she rang up Elizabeth Eckford to apologise. 'I am deeply ashamed of the photograph,' she said later, 'I was an immature 15-year-old. That's the way things were. I grew up in a segregated society and I thought that's the way it was and that's the way it should be.'

6 [ ] 'I wanted to end my identification as the poster child for the hate generation, trapped in the image captured in that photograph. I know my life was more than a moment.' And William Counts was there to take a new photograph of another moment – of reconciliation.

3 Who were the following people, what did they do and when did they do it?
The first one is done for you.

Name	Who?	What?	When?
Hazel Bryan	a white student at Little Rock's Central High School	b – shouted at a black student – apologised – reconciled with the black student	c – 1957 – 1962 – 1997
William Counts	d	e	f
Bill Clinton	g	h	i
Dwight D. Eisenhower	j	k	l
Orval Faubus	m	n	o
Elizabeth Eckford	p	q	r

Language in chunks

4 Match the phrases in italics from the text (a–g, on the left) with their explanations (1–7, on the right).

a *a fact of life* [ ]
b *bitterly opposed to* [ ]
c I can never *fully repay my debt to* [ ]
d *in the wake of* [ ]
e she never *lost her composure* [ ]
f *there would be trouble* [ ]
g to *change the course of history* [ ]

1 after (and as a result of) an event
2 make things different for ever
3 something that is or was always true
4 in strong disagreement with
5 something bad was going to happen
6 stopped looking calm
7 give someone what we think we owe them

5 Use the words in brackets to re-write the following sentences so that they mean more or less the same. Use the phrases in italics from Activity 4.

Example: a *She never lost her composure when the police arrested her.*

a She didn't seem to be upset when the police arrested her. (composure)
b Everybody gets colds and flu from time to time. (fact)
c Nothing was ever the same after the Industrial Revolution. (course)
d It is impossible to thank you enough. (debt)
e I am totally against your plan. (bitterly)
f They built new flood defences after the terrible storm. (wake)
g When he saw the people in the stadium, he knew things were going to go wrong. (trouble)

●●● B What cameras are used for

The Big Brother Site   The place where civil liberties are put to the test

HOME

BIG BROTHER IS
WATCHING YOU

THE GATSOMETER:
FRIEND OR FOE

SMILE! YOU'RE ON
CAMERA

ID CARDS – WHO IS
BEING PROTECTED
FROM WHOM

BBS MESSAGE BOARD

CONTACT US

Thank you Maurice Gatsonides?

Although most people do not know who Maurice Gatsonides was, almost all of us know about his most famous invention. It is used in over 35 countries worldwide. In Britain it is sometimes called the 'Gatsometer'.

Gatsonides was a Belgian rally driver who invented the speed cameras which you can see on motorways all over Europe, the Gulf region, North and South America and the Far East. The cameras are activated either by sensors on the surface of the road or by a radar device which picks up cars as they pass. Pictures of vehicles are taken less than half a second apart, and this tells the machine exactly how fast they are travelling.

Speeding – and attempts to control it – is not a modern phenomenon. For example, when the first 'horseless carriages' were introduced in Britain in the 19th century, they were not allowed to go faster than a walking pace. A man had to walk in front of these new vehicles with a red flag in order to protect the public. But all that changed in 1896 when the maximum speed limit was increased to 14 miles per hour (22.5 kph). That was too late for Londoner Walter Arnold, however. A few months before the new law came into effect, he had been fined a shilling (five pence) for driving at 8 miles an hour (nearly 13 kph), in a 2 mph speed limit area. He was caught by a policeman on a bicycle who chased him and brought him to justice.

Speed limits are faster now, from 50 mph (80 kph) on most US freeways to 70 mph (112 kph) on British motorways. Other countries set their own limits. In Germany, for example, the top autobahn speed limit is 130 kph. Yet people still die as a result of speeding, especially in built-up areas where the difference between being hit by a car at 20 mph and 30 mph is often the difference between injury and death. Speed cameras, in towns and on the open road, are designed to stop the big toll of injury and death on our roads. As such they are, surely, uncontroversial.

Or are they?

For and against

There are people who hate speed cameras. Some go even further and set cameras on fire or cover their lenses with black paint so that they do not work.

Among the arguments against speed cameras are that:

- Motorways are safe. Speed isn't the main cause of accidents.
- When speed cameras are visible – because they are painted in bright colours – drivers slow down. But many speed cameras are nearly invisible or hidden so their only function must be to make money for the police.
- People say that speed cameras have lowered the accident rate, but this could be due instead to better road surfaces, advances in vehicle design and better security measures (which means that not so many cars are stolen by young 'joyriders').

Yet, police forces around the world reply by saying that the results of experiments are quite clear. In Britain, for example, the first UK trial of a brightly painted 'Gatso' camera at a notorious black spot saw an 80 per cent reduction in injury and accidents. In towns, speeds have been cut and anyway, they point out, anything that saves even one life must be worth the effort.

What's your view? Do you love your Gatsometers or would you like to see them all torn up and thrown away? Contact us and join the debate.

1 Write the names or numbers in the space provided.

  a He invented speed cameras. ....

  b He was punished for going too fast. ....

  c the speed at which accidents are often fatal ....

  d the percentage by which accidents fell in a UK study ....

2 Match the sentences halves. The first one is done for you.

  a A man with a red flag   [9]   1 ... believe that speed cameras make the roads safer.
  b A policeman on a bicycle   [   ]   2 ... caught Walter Arnold driving too fast.
  c Police authorities around the world   [   ]   3 ... is a British nickname for speed cameras.
  d Some people believe that   [   ]   4 ... is the result of better car design and road surfacing rather than speed cameras.
  e Some people think that improved road safety   [   ]   5 ... of radars or road-based sensors.
  f Some protesters   [   ]   6 ... on German autobahns than on American freeways.
  g Speed cameras   [   ]   7 ... speed cameras which you can't see are just a way of getting money from drivers.
  h Speed cameras work because   [   ]   8 ... try to stop speed cameras working.
  i The Gatsometer   [   ]   9 ... used to walk in front of the first cars.
  j Walter Arnold   [   ]   10 ... was put at a black spot, the accident rate fell.
  k When a highly-visible speed camera   [   ]   11 ... was travelling 6 mph too fast.
  l You can drive faster   [   ]   12 ... were invented by the Belgian rally driver Maurice Gatsonides.

3 Complete each blank with one word or phrase from the text. Do not change it in any way.

  a The alarm was .... when the thief walked through a radar beam by mistake.

  b .... were placed on the patient's skin to measure temperature and heart rate.

  c When oil spills out of a ship, it remains on the .... of the water.

  d A biometric scanner is a .... for checking someone's identity.

  e The increase in the world's temperature is a .... that cannot be denied.

  f We call an area .... if there are many houses and shops there.

  g Years of playing American football have taken a heavy .... on his health, which is now poor.

  h We call something .... when we think that people are not likely to argue about it.

  i We call young people who steal cars and then drive them very fast just for fun ....

  j A .... is a place where more accidents happen than in many other places.

••C Summarising (newspaper headlines)

1 Look at these newspaper headlines and answer the questions.

a What is the story behind the headlines, do you think?
b What, typically, is left out in newspaper headlines? What verb tenses are common?

Shake-up in car-parking fees

Family 'owe lives' to smoke detector

Little Rock photographer dies at 70

Photo booth murder suspect arrested

Queen's horse in photo finish win

2 Read the following story. How many headlines can you write which summarise the story using some of the words in blue? (You may have to change some of the words, e.g. from verbs to nouns, etc.)

A mother of three escaped injury when the car she was driving plunged into a river. She had been driving home after dropping her children at school. She was rescued by a passing cyclist who dived into the river and pulled her from the car. 'I owe that man my life,' said Mrs Martha Galvan, 'he's a hero, but his identity is a mystery. He ran off after he had rescued me so I don't know who he is.'

Example: River plunge mother escapes injury

Compare your answers with the suggestions in the answer key on page 106.

....
....
....
....
....
....
....

3 Read the following stories and circle the words you may want to use in headlines which will summarise them.

When James Knight, a university student, went to collect his photographs at Boots 24-hour developing centre on Thursday, he got the shock of his life. Two of the photographs showed his girlfriend standing in a street in London. But behind her were two robbers running out of a bank. 'I didn't notice them at the time,' Knight said, 'but when I showed them to the police they were very excited.' The police have since made two arrests.

The Swedish singer Carla was making no comment yesterday after an incident at Mexico City Airport in which she hit out at a press photographer, breaking his nose. The attack took place as the singer was arriving from Sweden for a countrywide tour. Witnesses said that Carla posed for the waiting photographers with her 6-year-old daughter who was accompanying her, but when one photographer, American Brad Puttnam, kept taking photographs of the mother and daughter, the singer lashed out. Puttnam is threatening to sue. The singer's publicity aide says that Carla regrets the incident and just wants to be left alone.

4 Write as many headlines as you can for the stories. Get as much information in the headlines as possible. Compare your headlines with the suggestions in the answer key.

....
....
....
....
....
....
....
....

●●A Wolves

1 One of the following mini-paragraphs represents the view of the writer Peter Hedley about wolves. Which do you think it is?

a Wolves are savage predators who attack human beings. They hunt on their own and abandon their young at an early age.

b Wolves are hated by most humans, but in reality they are sociable animals who love singing, playing and dancing.

c In stories, wolves are always portrayed as dangerous and bad (as devils and werewolves) because of the way they behave in the wild.

d Wolves are beautiful beasts, but they make a terrible noise when there is a full moon.

Now read the text on the following page. Were you right?

2 Who or what:

a ... was the reason farmers didn't like wolves? ....

b ... is Little Red Riding Hood? ....

c ... is *Peter and the Wolf*? ....

d ... was the image of a wolf used for many years ago? ....

e ... do wolves use instead of frisbees? ....

f ... sometimes kills their own or their partner's children? ....

g ... killed his brother? ....

Language in chunks

3 Look at how these phrases are used in the text and then use them in the sentences which follow. You may have to change them a little to make them fit.

ashamed of themselves

for a start

get our hands on

in the end

just for the fun of it

they do their best

to keep out of our way

a Don't come anywhere near me. Just ....

b I didn't come yesterday because .... , after a long day, I just didn't have the energy.

c I don't mind if I pass or fail. I just want to ....

d I've always wanted to own one of Picasso's paintings. I'd love to .... one.

e Bungee-jumping isn't good for me or useful or anything. I do it ....

f Why do I want to leave my job? Well, ... , I'm not enjoying it any more. But there are many other reasons too.

g Why did you cheat in your exam? You should be ....

How could we get it so wrong?

Recent controversies over the reintroduction of wolves to parts of the United States and Scotland yet again focus on one of nature's most misunderstood beasts.
Peter Hedley takes up the story.

Once upon a time, much of the world was populated by wolves. They ranged all over the United States and Canada, Siberia and much of mainland Europe, as well as Great Britain, and if humans hadn't come along, they would still be there in great numbers. But man did come along, farmed the land, objected to the wolves killing their livestock and so gradually drove them out of the homes that had once been theirs.

Yet wolves are totally unlike the image we have of them from legend and language. For a start, they don't attack humans; indeed they do their best to keep out of our way. They are very sociable animals, living in packs and looking after their young with a fondness that should make some humans ashamed of themselves. Far from wolf music being ugly, the howl of the wolf – the cry of the whole pack - as the full moon rises in a star-bright sky is one of the most beautiful sounds in nature. Wolves dance and play games like frisbee and tag with bones and twigs. They are beautiful creatures which can run at speeds of up to 65 kph if they have to. They can jump vertically and run up rock faces like a cat. And when they do kill, their 42 large teeth, exerting a pressure of 1,500 lbs per square inch, are fearsomely effective.

Wolves are not victims in our language and our literature, however. In fairy stories, they are seen as evil and dangerous, always ready to eat people. Remember the time when Little Red Riding Hood thinks that a wolf is her grandmother? 'What big teeth you've got, grandmother!', she says, and the wolf, disguised as her grandmother, growls back sadistically, 'All the better to eat you with, my dear!' In Prokofiev's musical fable *Peter and the Wolf*, the old grandfather speaks for us all at the end when he says, 'Ah, but if Peter hadn't caught the wolf, what then?!'

In medieval times, the devil was often portrayed as a wolf, and the concept of a werewolf – the man who turns into a savage monster on the night of the full moon – is still a popular figure in both books and films.

If you really want to see how English-speaking humans think of the wolf, just look at the language! 'A wolf in sheep's clothing' is not a pleasant person and a 'wolf-whistle' is not a pleasant sound!

But the fact remains that we love the lion, the king of the jungle, another killer that spends much of its time asleep and often practises infanticide, while we demonise the wolf, one of the most beautiful animals in the world. Only occasionally do writers treat them nicely; for example, a she-wolf is supposed to have suckled the twins Remus and Romulus, who went on to found the city of Rome. If only the boys had stayed with her, perhaps they would have learnt to love and respect each other. But instead they went back to the human world, Romulus killed his brother and Rome was founded in rivers of blood.

And so, while man kills animals in their millions, often just for the fun of it, the wolf on the mountain, out in the wilderness, running over the Siberian wastes, represents a state of natural grace that we do not know and can never obtain, even though we dream of it in our hearts. Perhaps that's why, in the end, we hate the wolf so much – for having something we can never get our hands on.

●●B Surprise

1 Match the creatures with the pictures. Write the number on the line.

1 alien	9 koala bear
2 bat	10 ostrich
3 cow	11 sheep
4 crocodile	12 snake
5 dog	13 stallion
6 galah	14 wolf
7 goat	15 wombat
8 kangaroo	

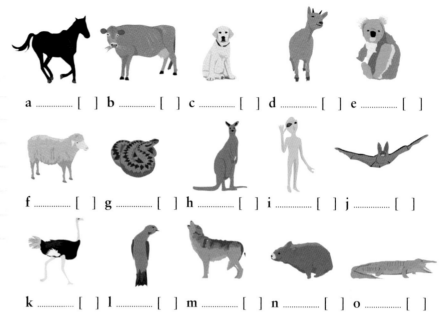

a .... [ ] b .... [ ] c .... [ ] d .... [ ] e .... [ ]

f .... [ ] g .... [ ] h .... [ ] i .... [ ] j .... [ ]

k .... [ ] l .... [ ] m .... [ ] n .... [ ] o .... [ ]

2 Read the text. Put a tick in the square brackets under the pictures if the creature is mentioned.

Kathryn Flett, a journalist living and working in London, describes going home to Australia unexpectedly.

I crept up to the back door, dodging some of the animals that might give me away: Eric the goat; Wylie, Trousers and Bo, the sheep; Murdoch, Pugsley, Benny and Nellie, the dogs; and Foster, the galah; while Don Carlos, the Arab stallion, snickered and eyed me warily as I eased open the door. At the end of the corridor my mother was sitting in the kitchen with a cup of coffee. She turned and stared. And stared. And carried on staring. Then her jaw really did drop. And after that there was some running and hugging and tears, and I thought: the 13,000 miles to Australia is a very long way to go to surprise your mother, but worth it.

My 16-year-old brother tried to be cool when we collected him from school (a 30-mile drive, half on dirt roads) but I've never seen him lost for words before. Last time I saw him at my wedding, he had a pudding-basin haircut and was the same height as me. Now an achingly handsome young guy with expensive tastes in go-faster footwear, he is 5ft 11 and growing. My runaway husband wouldn't stand a chance. Indeed when Johnny threatened to kneecap him, I was touched.

One night I helped Johnny with his homework, then, armed with a torch and camera, we went wombat-hunting. The stars were so bright it was like walking underneath a floodlit colander. We disturbed kangaroos and cows (which I mistook for aliens; easily done) but wombats remained elusive. After about an hour of my brother helping me over fences and saying things like, 'if you see a snake, keep perfectly still,'

we sat on a boulder for a rest. There was a rustling noise a few feet away. I aimed the lens vaguely in the right direction and shot.

'Betcha goddit!' said Johnny. While I betted that I hadn't, we ambled back to the house via the dam, where tiny wombat footprints could be seen in the mud.

'Find any?' asked my mother.

'No. But we did get abducted by cows,' I said. Johnny giggled as we both slumped in front of the television and our mother cooked us dinner, which I love because it happens so rarely.

I was in Australia for nine days and it wasn't long enough. Most of the time I mooched around looking miserable about my divorce and then apologising for it. I didn't want to talk about it. I just wanted my dinner cooked and my washing done and to stay up late watching bad telly.

While I was waiting for the 8.15 from Golburn station to take me to Sydney to catch a plane to Bali, to catch a plane to Kuala Lumpur, to catch a plane to London, our friend took a picture of Mummy, Johnny and I beneath the station clock. At Sydney airport I had time to kill so I got the film processed. The group shot under the clock was delightful. God knows when we'll have another one done, but I know that Johnny will be even taller.

Incidentally, there was no wombat, just aliens.

3   Answer the following questions with 'yes' or 'no', and say how you know.

   a Was Kathryn's mother surprised to see her? How do you know?

   ....

   b Was Kathryn's brother surprised to see her? How do you know?

   ....

   c Was Kathryn's husband with her? How do you know?

   ....

   d Had Kathryn's brother changed since she had last seen him? How do you know?

   ....

   e Was it a dark night when they went out wombat-hunting? How do you know?

   ....

   f Did Kathryn and her brother take a gun? How do you know?

   ....

   g Did Kathryn take any successful photographs? How do you know?

   ....

   h Was Kathryn pleased to be at home? How do you know?

   ....

   i Did Kathryn get a direct flight back to London? How do you know?

   ....

4   Read the sentences (a–n) and then write the number of the correct
    definition (1–17) of the words in blue at the end of each sentence.

   a I crept up to the back door, dodging some ....
      animals that might give me away.   ....

   b Then her jaw really did drop.   ....

   c And after that there was some running
      and hugging and tears.   ....

   d I've never seen him lost for words before. ....

   e He had a pudding-basin haircut.   ....

   f My runaway husband wouldn't stand a
      chance.   ....

   g Indeed when Johnny threatened to
      kneecap him, I was touched.   ....

   h It was like walking underneath a
      (1) floodlit (2) colander.   ....

   i Wombats remained elusive.   ....

   j I aimed the lens vaguely in the right
      direction and shot.   ....

   k We did get abducted by cows.   ....

   l Johnny giggled as we both slumped   ....
      in front of the television.

   m I mooched around looking miserable.   ....

   n I had time to kill.   ....

   1 a metal bowl with a lot of holes used for
      drying salad, spaghetti, etc.
   2 difficult to find
   3 embracing
   4 half lay, half sat
   5 her mouth opened in surprise
   6 laughed quickly in a high voice
   7 moved around with no real purpose
   8 moved in a 'secret' quiet way
   9 nothing much to do for a period
   10 old-fashioned like an upside-down cooking
      dish
   11 shoot someone in the knees as a punishment
   12 survive / be successful
   13 taken away, kidnapped
   14 tell someone that I was there even though it
      was a secret
   15 took a photograph
   16 unable to speak because of surprise
   17 with a bright light shone on it

•• C Linking words and phrases

1 a Read the question opposite and the student composition which answered it. Is the student generally in favour of zoos or not?

Write a composition discussing the statement.

b In formal writing, we use more sophisticated words than *and*, *but* and *so*. Replace the words in blue in the student's composition with the following words and phrases. Use each one once only.

as a result

and furthermore

however

in conclusion

therefore

in contrast

moreover

not only that, but

nevertheless

on the other hand

Discuss this statement:

Nobody should enjoy going to zoos which keep animals in cages.

I'd like to start this composition by saying that I have enjoyed going to zoos and looking at animals in the past. It's always very exciting to look at creatures you have never seen before. .... But many people say that zoos are not pleasant places .... and the animals are in cages and don't have their freedom. .... And if you deny animals their freedom and keep them in enclosed spaces, they become ill and psychologically disturbed.

.... But people who support zoos say that the animals are well looked after and fed, something that does not always happen to them in the wild. .... And zoos have started many breeding programmes to save endangered species. .... So many animals that might have become extinct are now still alive.

If I had thought about it when I first went to see a zoo, I would have been unhappy about animals in cages, and I now think that is wrong. .... But some of the wildlife parks in various countries in the world give animals both security and freedom. .... So those are the ones I approve of.

.... So I think that zoos are often cruel places. Proper wildlife parks are a better way for man to preserve species whilst, at the same time, giving us all a chance to see animals in a natural habitat. .... But I am sure many families will still take their young children to visit zoos.

Notes:
• *However* is generally followed by a comma. When it occurs in the middle of a sentence, it has a comma before it too.
• *Moreover* generally occurs at the beginning of a sentence or a clause (e.g. after a semi-colon). In the middle of sentences, it usually occurs with *and* and has commas before and after it (... *and, moreover, ...*)

2 Read the following composition question.

Zoos are absolutely vital for the protection of various animal species.

Make notes in English for and against the opinion given.

3 Plan your own composition (three or four paragraphs).

Paragraph 1: introduce the topic. (*I'd like to start by ...*)
Paragraph 2: set out arguments / give reasons.
Paragraph 3: set out more arguments / give more reasons.
Paragraph 4: draw your own conclusion. (*In conclusion, therefore, ...*)

4 Write your composition, using some or all of the linkers from Activity 1b.

...A Looking danger in the face

1 Read about the two people and complete the table.

	Text 1	Text 2
a Name of main character		
b Date and place of birth of main character		
c What the main character does		
d What is special about what he / she does		
e How the main character started		
f Achievements (if listed)		
g Any other interesting information		

1

American-born Dustin Webster has loved high-diving ever since his parents took him to see high-divers at an amusement park in San Diego when he was 11. He went backstage to ask the divers how they did it and six years later he joined their team. He has been high-diving ever since.

The kind of diving Dustin does is called cliff diving, and it's not like the diving you see in the Olympics. For a start, the distance from the board to the water (about 25 metres) is much greater than that. And secondly, cliff divers like Dustin do triple and quadruple somersaults on the way down. This makes cliff diving highly skilled and extremely dangerous. Many of them suffer injury and, on occasions, death if they land in the water on their stomachs or their backs. 'From 25 metres up, you fall a bit like a grand piano,' Dustin says cheerfully. They have been known to break their legs if they land on a fish or a piece of seaweed.

When you watch cliff divers, you get a real sense of how absolutely terrifying it is. They stand on the edge of the board and look down, far far down, and then they launch themselves twisting into the air. No matter how many times you do it, Dustin and his colleagues say, you never lose the fear just before you jump.

So how come Colombian Orlando Duque, who has just beaten Dustin to become the latest cliff diving champion, looked so still and God-like as he stood above a seawater lake in Greece, arms outstretched, his long black hair falling down his back, protected by nothing except a small pair of red swimming trunks? That day, back in July, he looked more like the statue of Christ in Rio de Janeiro than a frail human being. And then he was gone, falling through the air, doing his famous back loop with four twists, incredibly graceful and frighteningly vulnerable. And it worked. When that day's competition was over, Duque had won the prize.

2

When world champion Francisco 'Pipin' Ferreras went to Baja California in 1996 to try and break the world freediving record he did not realise that he would meet the young woman who would soon become his wife. But that is what happened, for she had been doing a university thesis on freediving and he was the one person she wanted to talk to about it. Audrey Mestre, the woman doing the thesis, was born in France on August 11, 1974. Her grandfather and her mother were both spearfishers and, as a result, Audrey had been diving since she was a child. She won her first swimming race when she was two-and-a-half years old and began scuba-diving when she was 13.

In 1990 she moved (with her family) to Mexico, and it was there that she started freediving – diving with no breathing apparatus, something that people who fish with spears have been doing for as long as there have been people living by the sea. But modern freedivers try to break world records all the time to see who can go deepest, and for how long, without any oxygen at all.

Pipin Ferreras is a world champion and pretty soon his new girlfriend (Audrey, soon to be his wife) was joining him in his record attempts. In 1997 she did a free dive of 80 metres and in 1998 she dived to 115 metres with her husband. Things really took off in May 2000, however, when off the coast of the Canary islands she broke the female freediving world record by reaching a depth of 125 metres and coming back in two minutes and three seconds. Only one year later, she reached 130 metres.

But freediving is a dangerous sport. On October 12, 2002, Audrey was in the Dominican Republic attempting to beat a record set by UK freediver Tanya Streeter. This time she went too far and she died.

2 Look at these sentences from the texts. What parts of speech are the words in blue? What words or phrases can replace the words in blue without changing the meaning too much?

a Then they launch themselves twisting into the air.

....

b They have been known to break their legs if they land ... on a piece of seaweed.

....

c He looked more like the statue ... than a frail human being.

....

d And then he was gone ... incredibly graceful and frighteningly vulnerable.

....

e She had been doing a university thesis on freediving.

....

f She ... began scuba-diving when she was 13.

....

g Freediving [means] diving with no breathing apparatus.

....

● ● ● B The safest hobby in the world?

Train-spotting – *the hobby*

Looking at the practice that has NOTHING to do with the movie.

1
Many people around the world have seen Danny Boyle's movie *Trainspotting** based on Irvine Welsh's novel of the same name and starring Ewan McGregor, but how many of us can really claim to know what train-spotting is all about? Now this is not considered the coolest hobby in town and the word 'train-spotter' in Britain has become synonymous with 'geek' or 'nerd', but is this reputation really deserved?

2
First of all, let's define train-spotting. There are said to be some 100,000 train-spotters in the UK. What do they do? Well, exactly as the title suggests, they spot trains, that is, they stand in train stations, look at the serial numbers of the trains that leave and arrive and write them down. The ultimate aim is to have seen every train in the country.

3
Being obsessed with railways and trains is not a modern hobby and dates back to 1804 when Richard Trevithick built the first steam locomotive, which hauled a load of ten tons of iron, 70 men and five wagons along a nine-mile stretch of track in two hours. As the number of trains grew and they got faster and faster, so did the interest in them grow. Is this any stranger than people who love cars?

4
So, what do you need to be a train-spotter? Well, it's a wonderfully inexpensive pastime – all you really need is a pen or pencil and a notebook to write down the train numbers. Other optional equipment includes hot tea in a thermos flask, a camera and some sandwiches for those long afternoons spent on train platforms when you don't want to risk the delights of railway station food. The modern train-spotter may also carry binoculars and a video camera, but for the purists these are unnecessary.

5
It's interesting to note that despite the stigma of train-spotting, there have been famous railway enthusiasts in history, such as the poet WH Auden, the comedian Michael Palin and, of course, Alfred Hitchcock, who was obsessed with trains and featured them regularly in his films, especially *The 39 Steps*. There is evidence, too, that being a train-spotter is not necessarily a peculiarly British hobby.

6
One glance at the array of US train sites should be enough to convince you that transatlantic train-spotters are alive and well. In America, they try to call rail enthusiasts 'trainfans' and talk of 'trainfanning'. Don't let this fool you – these people are train-spotters and there are a lot of them. Each month, two million pages are visited on the website TrainWeb.org. And you may also be interested in the distant, more athletic relative of the trainfanner – those daredevil types who inhabit the illegal world of freight train-hopping.

7 *So call them 'nerds' or 'geeks', but they are here to stay and this is certainly not a hobby that is violent or dangerous in any way, nor does it cause any kind of damage to the environment. What do you think is healthier – sitting in front of a TV screen and criticising those who do something that doesn't interest you? Or going out and finding and following your passion whatever that happens to be? I know what I think.*

*Train-spotting can be written with or without a hyphen.

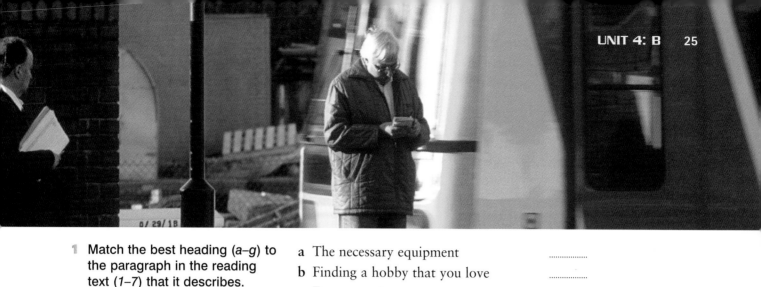

1 Match the best heading (*a–g*) to the paragraph in the reading text (*1–7*) that it describes.

a The necessary equipment ....
b Finding a hobby that you love ....
c Famous train-spotters ....
d Train-spotting in the USA ....
e What is train-spotting? ....
f The book, the film and the pastime ....
g The origins of the hobby ....

2 Are these statements *True* or *False* according to the text? Write T or F in the brackets.

a There is a famous movie which is about the hobby. [ ]
b Train-spotting is a very cool hobby. [ ]
c The objective of train-spotting is to see as many trains as possible. [ ]
d The author thinks it is strange to be interested in cars. [ ]
e It does not cost a lot of money to be a train-spotter. [ ]
f All train-spotters use binoculars. [ ]
g There are no images of trains in the movie *The 39 Steps*. [ ]
h In the USA, train-spotters have a different name. [ ]
i It is against the law to get on and ride a goods train. [ ]
j The author thinks train-spotting is a worthless hobby. [ ]

3 Look at the way the following words and phrases are used in the text and then write them in the gaps (*a–h*).

daredevil

freight

obsessed with

stigma

synonymous with

thermos flask

transatlantic

ultimate

a He takes a lot of risks in his car. He's a .... when it comes to driving.
b She took some coffee with her in a .... and it was still hot when she drank it at lunchtime.
c In some situations, *light* is .... 'not heavy', but sometimes it can mean the opposite of *dark*.
d He doesn't know whether he can re-sit his exam: he is waiting for the school's .... decision.
e She watches movies all the time and talks about them. She is .... cinema.
f There are no passengers allowed on that ship. It's for .... only.
g There is a .... attached to being an ex-convict even though that person has been punished and has paid their debt to society.
h I have a meeting in New York next week so I'm taking a .... flight on Sunday.

••C Email interview

1 Read the email interview. Most of the questions are missing. Match the questions with the answers.

a How do you relax? ....

b How would you like to be remembered? ....

c What is the most important lesson life has taught you? ....

d What is your greatest fear? ....

e What is your greatest regret? ....

f What is your idea of perfect happiness? ....

g What language do you overuse most often? ....

h What three words best describe you? ....

i Which living person would you most like to go on a date with? ....

j Who or what is the greatest love of your life? ....

The email interview

Twenty-three-year-old Emma Sanchez is a paraski champion. Paraskiing, whether on snow or on water, uses a small parachute to pull the skier along.

Emma lives in Detroit with her family, but she spends a lot of her time paraskiing off beaches all over the world, especially in Mexico, her parents' native land. Both her brothers have won titles as barefoot skiers, but Emma still prefers the parachute.

What is your most vivid childhood memory?
When my Dad took me water-skiing for the first time in Acapulco. We were in Mexico for a holiday with my grandparents. All I was told was 'shut up and hold on!'.

1 Enrique Iglesias – because he's got the best voice, he's good looking and he's like me, he lives in two cultures.

2 Fit, funny, beautiful (only joking about the last one!).

3 I think I say 'like, whatever' all the time. At least that's what my friends and family tell me!

4 A bright blue morning, a strong wind and a gently rolling sea.

5 That I'll break something and not be able to paraski anymore.

6 My family, especially my two brothers Paco and Raymundo.

7 That I didn't work harder at school.

8 I go to nightclubs, movies, just hang out with my friends.

9 As someone who loved life. But I'm not going anywhere yet!

10 There's no point in doing anything unless you put your whole heart into it.

2 The email interviewer could have asked the questions differently.
Match these new questions (*a–j*) with answers (*1–10*) in the interview.

a Do you have any annoying habits? ....

b How do you want people to think about you in the future? ....

c How would you describe yourself? ....

d Is there anything that you are sorry about in your life? ....

e What are you most afraid of? ....

f What do you do in your free time? ....

g What is a perfect day for you? ....

h What is your philosophy in life? ....

i Who or what is the most important thing in your life? ....

j Who would you most like to go out with? ....

3 Now choose ten of the questions from Activities 1 and 2 that you like best and ask a friend or relative to answer them by email.

4 Finally, write up your friend's or relative's answers like the email interview with Emma.

●●A What's anger all about?

1 Underline words and phrases in *The anger page* which tell you that the following statements are true. The first one is underlined for you.

a Anger is often a reaction to some other feeling.
b We often shout to get rid of other feelings.
c Anger may be the result of some particular brain activity.
d Family background may affect how angry we are.
e We think anger is bad for us.
f Controlling anger may be harmful.
g We should try to be in charge of our own anger.

THE ANGER PAGE

What is anger?

Anger has many sources. Often it is an emotion which is <u>secondary to some other emotion</u> that you are feeling – like fear, guilt or relief. So the parent who shouts at her kid who gets home late is using anger as a way of displacing fear. Sometimes it is the result of a sense of great unfairness – such as when someone is wrongly accused of a crime, or finds that their partner has not been telling them the truth, or feels a passionate sense of social injustice.

But anger may have other causes as well. We know that animals can be made more aggressive if the limbic parts of their brains are stimulated; thus overstimulation of the limbic (emotional) centre of the brain may override the neocortex (the reasoning part).

Changes in hormone levels seem to cause anger too, and inheritance plays a part, as does our upbringing. The more we are raised in anger, the more anger we are likely to feel later in our lives.

Is anger bad for you?

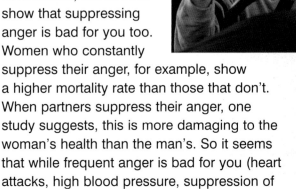

Most researchers think that chronic anger leads to an increased risk of heart attack, but studies show that suppressing anger is bad for you too. Women who constantly suppress their anger, for example, show a higher mortality rate than those that don't. When partners suppress their anger, one study suggests, this is more damaging to the woman's health than the man's. So it seems that while frequent anger is bad for you (heart attacks, high blood pressure, suppression of the immune system), the suppression of anger is worse.

Some commentators suggest that using anger consciously is a good thing, provided it is not too extreme or out of control, but others are convinced that anger could be one of the main factors controlling our emotional and physical health.

Differences between men and women   Dealing with anger

Home | About Us | Subjects A – Z | Contact Us | Behaviour modification classes | Search

2 Follow the link to *Differences between men and women* and then answer *True* or *False* to statements *a–f*.

Differences between men and women

Home

About Us

Subjects A – Z

Contact Us

Behaviour modification classes

Search

The anger page

Dealing with anger

Studies have long shown differences between the way men and women react, how they use anger, and how anger affects them. However, this may be changing as society changes.

We do know that by the age of three, boys show three times as much aggressive behaviour as girls do, and that high levels of testosterone (the male hormone) have been linked with increased anger patterns. So it does seem that men, in general, are 'angrier' than women.

Anger is also more acceptable in men than in women. Those women who show anger are often thought of as mad, bad, crazy and emotional. Studies suggest that many women in such situations suppress their anger or channel it in other ways such as eating disorders, for example. It is now thought that suppressing anger is extremely bad for people, especially women.

However, in the eyes of many researchers, the difference between the sexes may not be nearly as significant as changes in society which have led to an erosion of social skills in both men and women. In the modern world, we spend more time on the Internet or looking at TV, and not enough time talking to each other. We expect everything to happen quickly and as a result we become frustrated very easily.

True or False?

a At three years old, there is no difference between the anger of boys and girls.   [ ]

b We are less likely to criticise men for being angry than we are to criticise women for being angry.   [ ]

c Eating too much or too little is sometimes a sign of anger in women.   [ ]

d It is better not to let your anger out.   [ ]

e Television can have a bad effect on the way we communicate with each other.   [ ]

f People who work on the Internet are more patient and don't get so angry.   [ ]

3 Follow the link to *Dealing with anger* and complete the tasks which follow.

Dealing with anger

Home | About Us | Subjects A – Z | Contact Us | Behaviour modification classes | Search

Here are some ways of dealing with anger.

Change what you expect. If you don't expect too much, you won't be too disappointed. If you are more flexible about what you want and need, you are less likely to become angry when the situation doesn't match up to your expectations.

Empathise with the other person. Try and understand his or her position. Why are they behaving like that? How would you feel if you were in their shoes? Can you sympathise with their reasons for being angry? Once you see things from their perspective, your anger may be replaced by concern.

Learn how to be assertive rather than aggressive. Being able to state a point of view or hold down an argument is different from shouting at someone.

Monitor your thoughts for traces of cynicism and general discontent. Then, when they come along, you're ready for them and you can minimise their effects.

Stop the clock. When you get angry, take a deep breath and stop the thoughts that are making you that way. Think of something pleasant instead, something you like and enjoy. Your anger will gradually lessen.

Surround yourself with positive people. The more people around you show that they are calm and happy, the calmer and happier you will become.

Use your imagination, not your voice. Imagine doing something terrible to the person who is annoying you, and channel all your anger into your imagination. That way, you are free to act calmly and rationally on the surface.

The anger page

Differences between men and women

Write the headings (e.g. 'Change what you expect') from *Dealing with anger* **next to the appropriate summaries.**

a Be strong, but not cross...

....

b Put yourself in the other person's shoes...

....

c Stay with people who aren't angry..

....

d Think about what you are thinking..

....

e Think something rather than do it..

....

f Learn to be satisfied with something a bit different.....................

....

g Wait until you are less angry...

....

Language in chunks

4 **Complete the sentences with these phrases from the three web pages (pages 28–30). You may have to change the phrases a little.**

| as a way of |
| bad for you |
| on the surface |
| out of control |
| plays a part |
| take a deep breath |
| use your imagination |

a When we want people to think a bit more creatively, we often say '...............................'.

b If you .... in a situation, it means you are there and you do things in that situation, though not necessarily the most important things.

c Everyone knows that smoking is ...., but they still go on doing it.

d If someone is ...., it means it will be difficult to quieten them down or restrain them.

e We describe something .... doing something if it is just one method of doing it.

f When you ...., you fill your lungs with air once – and perhaps it gives you time to think.

g Some people can look calm ...., but actually, inside, they're feeling very angry.

●●● B   Smiling and frowning

1 Read *Notes & Queries*. Who:

a ... doesn't know how people discovered poisonous foods?

....

b ... has a question about animals?

....

c ... makes a comment about white teeth?

....

d ... suggests that smiling actually makes you happier?

....

e ... is worried about how they are going to look later on?

....

f ... says that you have to smile with your eyes if you want it to be genuine?

....

g ... makes a joke about scientists?

....

h ... suggests that smiling is easier because we get a lot of smiling practice?

....

i ... thinks that smiling is sometimes difficult?

....

j ... wants to know whether smiling is easier than frowning?

....

k ... is depressed about the reaction of other people?

....

l ... has a question about sports?

....

Notes & Queries

I have heard that it takes many more muscles to frown than to smile. Is it true, and does that mean that smiling is easier?
Phil Discarson, Preston, England

It's only easier if you have something to smile about. Otherwise it's almost impossible!   *Katie Davis, Canterbury, UK*

I read on a website (www.straightdope.com) that the opposite is true. According to someone called Doctor Song, a plastic surgeon, you use 12 main muscles for a genuine 'zygomatic' smile, but only 11 for a frown. But he says that even though we use more muscles to smile, it's actually easier because, since we smile more often than we frown, our smiling muscles are in better condition.   *Carl Preston, San Francisco, USA*

If scientists have been studying how many muscles it takes to smile and frown, it shows they have way too much free time on their hands, but since they've told us, we'd better all do a lot of frowning since it burns more calories.   *Bob Cartwright, Johannesburg, South Africa*

It depends what you mean by smiling. Remember that line from Shakespeare, 'a man may smile and smile and be a villain' – I think it's from his play *Hamlet*. Anyone can look as if they are smiling by using the *zygomaticus major* and *minor* (they pull up the corners of the mouth), the *levator labii superioris* (which pull up the mouth and the corners of the nose) and the *risorius* (which pulls the corner of the mouth to one side). But that's not a real smile. A real smile uses the *orbicularis oculi* which encircle each eye and so when you smile like this, these muscles tighten the skin round the eye to give that 'crinkling' effect which creates 'laughter' lines. That's a REAL smile!
Sarah Green (Dr), Birmingham, UK

Smiling or frowning, who cares?! They both give you lines when you're older so my advice is to avoid doing them completely. Especially when you're young.   *Miriam Sterling, Aberdeen, Scotland*

Counting the muscles it takes to smile and frown isn't the issue, for me. I am more interested in the fact that you can find examples of the saying that 'it takes less effort to smile than to frown' as far back as the 19th century. That's because it's a piece of advice, not a scientific fact. 'Smile, and the world smiles with you' is another saying like that. Others say that if you smile, you will almost always feel happier. So which comes first, the smile or the happiness?
   Well I just read some research which said that when we smile (or frown), our bodies get the message, even if we are only pretending. Apparently they got some people to pretend to be angry, sad, disgusted, etc., and use the appropriate facial expressions, and measured what happened to their bodies. And the incredible thing was that even though the test subjects knew they were acting, their bodies didn't. Their heart rates increased, their skin temperature got hotter and there were signs of sweating – all physical manifestations of real anger, etc.
Felicity Poole, Amsterdam, Holland

Home

Recent queries

Send a query

Any answers?

I don't know about smiling and frowning, but when I tell jokes, nobody laughs. What's the scientific explanation for that?
Danuta Ross, Penzance, UK

It may be easier, but whether it is nicer depends on your dentist!
Bud Karlowski, Portland, USA

QUERIES

Why don't cats like dogs?
Hugh Foster, London, UK

Why do football teams have 11 players?
Caroline Hartley, Melbourne, Australia

Why is English spelling so confusing?
Sergio Cardenas, Barranquilla, Colombia

What will happen when all the traffic in the country grinds to a halt?
Martin Goodman, Cambridge, UK

How did early humans decide which plants were OK to eat?
Petra Weiss, Basel, Switzerland

2 **Look again at the text and answer the following questions.**

a Where does the text come from?

b Which answers are serious?

c Which answers are not meant to be serious?

d Tick the following opinions if you find them in *Notes & Queries*.

1 We frown more than we smile.   [ ]
2 We smile more than we frown.   [ ]
3 Frowning must be a good form of exercise. [ ]
4 Laughter lines are good.   [ ]
5 Laughter lines are bad.   [ ]
6 When you smile nobody smiles back.   [ ]
7 No one can tell if your smile is genuine. [ ]

3 **Complete the sentences with the following words and phrases from the text.**

appropriate facial expressions   as far back as   burn calories

depends on   free time   get the message   in better condition

laughter lines   physical manifestations   pretending   tell jokes

villain

a If someone is fitter than they were, we can say that they are
....

b If the teacher is the person who decides if you can go to the next class, we say that it .... the teacher.

c If we say that something took place a long time in the past (say in the 17th century), we can say that it happened .... 1657.

d If you want to make people believe something is true, you are .... that it is true.

e If you change the look of your face to show different emotions, you use ....

f If you understand what someone is trying to say to you, you ....

g Raised heart rate and sweating are .... of fear.

h The lines at the sides of people's eyes are often called ....

i The main bad character in a story is often called the ....

j The time when we are not working or doing some other obligatory activity is ....

k When we transform the food we have eaten into energy by taking exercise, we ....

l When you .... , you try and make people laugh.

••C Designing leaflets

1 Look at the leaflet for *Aroma* and complete the table about it.

Aroma staff:

Sally Grace NAL, director

Justin Knocker, FSDE

Helena Kollect, CCE

Contact Aroma at:
The Aroma Centre
26 Carper Row Middleton Cleethorpe
Lancs LT6 5YW Tel: 01672 462057
Email: enquiries@arofengcol.com
Website: www.arofengcol.com

AROMA
Using nature's gift to keep you calm

AROMA

Courses in

AROMATHERAPY
• How different smells affect our mood
• Designing aroma zones
• Judging the best aromas on the market

FENG SHUI*
• The theory of Feng Shui explained
• Putting Feng Shui into practice at home
• Putting Feng Shui into practice at work

RELAXING COLOUR
• How colour affects our mood
• Colour combinations
• Designing rooms with colour in mind

Feng Shui is the ancient Chinese science which tells people the best place to put furniture in a room or house for maximum comfort and success.

	Description and details
Name of the place described	*Aroma*
What kind of a place is it? (Explain this in your own words.)	
Services offered (Give brief explanations in your own words.)	
Names of the staff	
Address, phone number, website, etc.	
How many sheets make up the leaflet? Do you think it is effective?	

2 Read the description and details for the organisation *Music Works* and complete the leaflet which follows.

	Description and details
Name of the place described	*Music Works*
What kind of a place is it?	It's a friendly family-based place where anyone who's interested in music can come along and play music, learn about music or just enjoy listening to it.
Services offered (and brief explanations of what these services are)	• Music appreciation classes for all ages (course on music and emotion, music styles through the ages, from classical to techno – styles and similarities). • Classes on a range of different instruments (from beginners to intermediate level on a variety of instruments, both classical and jazz or pop-based). • You can join one of three orchestras (classical strings, jazz orchestra, folk ensemble). • Concerts every Saturday.
Names of the staff	• Sebastian West (string tutor: violin, viola, cello, guitar) • Kylie Strachan (saxophone and jazz tutor / jazz orchestra conductor) • Christopher Major (understanding music / folk ensemble coach) • David Jones (string orchestra conductor)
Address, phone number, website, etc.	175 Harbour Walk, Lowminster LH3 5YT tel: 017583 444456 email: info@muswork.org.uk And there's a website at www.muswork.org.uk

Music Works

Music Works staff:

a ....

b ....

c ....

d ....

Contact *Music Works* at:

e ....

f ....

Tel: g ....

Email: h ....

Website: i ....

Activities:

• j ....

• k ....

• l ....

• m ....

••A What kind of future?

1 **Read the text and match the titles (*a–h*) to the paragraphs (*1–8*). The first one is done for you.**

a	Making it a place where we can live	[7]
b	Operations at a distance	[ ]
c	Finding a new place to live	[ ]
d	Right *and* wrong about the future	[ ]
e	His predictions are based on fact	[ ]
f	Grow your own new body parts?	[ ]
g	Less than 100 years away	[ ]
h	A top doctor makes predictions	[ ]

2 **Answer these questions based on the text.**

a Why was von Neumann both right *and* wrong?

....

b What are the two developments that mean we could now potentially grow a new limb?

....

....

c What was so unusual about the gall bladder operation in 2001?

....

d Why would humans die on Mars?

....

e How could Mars be made habitable for humans?

....

....

f How soon could we live on Mars, according to McKay?

....

3 **Match these words in the text to their meaning.**

a	foresees (paragraph 2)	1	describing, making a plan of	[ ]
b	leading (paragraph 3)	2	making or doing something faster	[ ]
c	mapping (paragraph 3)			
d	reconstructive (paragraph 3)	3	no longer existing	[ ]
e	fanciful (paragraph 4)	4	most important, most respected	[ ]
f	extinct (paragraph 6)	5	predicts, sees in the future	[ ]
g	shortcutting (paragraph 7)	6	impossible, imaginary	[ ]
		7	recreating or rebuilding	[ ]

Wings, babies and the pollution of planets

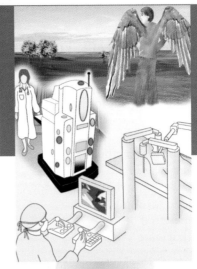

Predicting the future has always been a risky business, but recent claims are almost literally unbelievable. Or are they?

Back in 1949, the scientist Johan von Neumann made a statement which was both extraordinarily wrong and profoundly correct. 'It would appear,' he wrote, 'that we have reached the limits of what it is possible to achieve with computer technology, although I should be careful with such statements, as they tend to sound pretty silly in five years.' How true! Looking into the future has always been a dangerous occupation.

William Futrell isn't afraid to make predictions, however. As one of America's top plastic surgeons, he foresees a time when people will be flying around using their own wings, men will be having babies, and when we lose a leg in an accident the hospital will just grow a new one for us – using our own DNA.

You can't dismiss Futrell's predictions as pure fantasy, not given the fact that he is one of the leading authorities in his field. He has trained at least 20 professors and directors of US medical institutions. 'What's changed,' he says, 'is that we're mapping the human genome, the code for all life. And we can now extract stem cells for this kind of reconstructive work from a person's adipose tissue' (that's fat, to you and me).

When people dismiss Futrell's ideas as fanciful, he points out how far we've come. At the hospital where he works, robots take X-rays and other medical supplies to and from the wards; in Florida, in 2001, a doctor operated on a patient by remote control for the first time. Using computers and the Internet, he removed the gall bladder of a woman in France, 3,500 miles away. These things were once unimaginable.

And now, perhaps, we'll be able to grow wings and replace any body parts which become old or damaged. 'Believe me,' Futrell says, 'wings are not a long way off.' And he means it.

But even if we learn how to cure our bodies and end up living for ever, there isn't anything we can do about the fact that one day, as the sun gets hotter, this Earth will be an uncomfortable place to live. According to astronomical engineer Robert Zubrin, the Earth will become extinct 'unless we bring Earth life out with us into the universe'. And the only place to go is Mars – it has water, carbon dioxide and nitrogen. But at the moment it is too cold and dry for human habitation. We'd die within seconds of stepping onto its surface. So we'll just have to do something about it.

'The first step to making Mars habitable is to warm it up,' says NASA scientist Chris McKay. His plan is to drop off a pollution-making machine that will scoot around the surface of the planet spewing out greenhouse gasses, thus shortcutting the slow process of evolution. The next step is oxygen – and what better oxygen-makers have we got than trees?

McKay predicts that we'll be living on Mars some time in the next 80 years. 'By that time,' he says, 'the planet will have its algae and bacteria, and we'll have planted forests of trees. It'll be just right for human habitation.' The only problem is that we won't all fit. Mars is only a tenth the size of Earth.

Language in chunks

4   **Look at how these phrases are used in the text on page 37 and then use them in the
    sentences which follow. You may have to change them a little to make them fit.**

tend to
to dismiss something as
a long way off
to warm something up
to scoot around
to spew out
by that time

a I don't think we'll be living on the Moon in the near future – I think
   that's still ....

b We need to .... these vegetables in the microwave before
   we can eat them.

c Mars might be habitable by the year 2100, but .... most of
   us won't be alive anymore.

d I can't believe you .... that idea .... foolish.
   I think it's a great idea.

e My mother just bought a new bicycle so that she can .... town
   to do her shopping.

f Most people .... think that doctors have to be present to
   perform an operation, but that's not necessarily true.

g The old car was .... clouds of smoke when I saw it at the side
   of the motorway.

5   **Write five predictions that are made in the text on page 37.**

a ....

b ....

c ....

d ....

e ....

••B Finding out about the future

1 Match the name of the text type to the US website extract (*1–6*).

a an advertisement for a book   [ ]
b a weather forecast   [ ]
c an advertisement for a fortune-teller [ ]
d a horoscope   [ ]
e part of a city guide to events   [ ]
f an advertisement for a science exhibition [ ]

①

Event Overview

See how information technology is rapidly transforming enterprise operations, the e-entertainment industry and business e-marketing strategies around the world. This event brings IT professionals together in a forum of knowledge exchange and networking to advance the IT industry. International experts will speak about the direction of the IT industry and share practical knowledge on the latest technological innovations and current business and management issues. Technology vendors will showcase the newest innovations of the industry. IT decision-makers will find that perfect business and technology solution for their enterprise. The **IT WorldExpo** is where the IT community converges.

②
Fri 11 **Takes and Out-takes from the Andy Warhol Museum** *Ronald Feldman Fine Arts Tue–Sat 10am–6pm; Mon by appointment.*
The gallery hosts an exhibit of art and archival material from the Prince of Pop to celebrate the Andy Warhol Museum's tenth anniversary. Thu 10–Jul 30.

Sun 13 **60 contemporary Chinese artists** *Asia Society* **and** *International Center of Photography Tue–Sun 11am–6pm; Fri 11am–9pm. $7, students and seniors $5, children under 16 accompanied by an adult and members free; Fri 6–9pm free.*
An avant-garde community began brewing in China at the end of the Cultural Revolution in 1976, and things really got cooking in the 1990s, when a new generation dealing with issues of identity, modernity and tradition turned to photography and video. The work of 60 contemporary Chinese artists is now on view at the Asia Society and ICP. Zhang Dali, Liu Zheng and Lin Tianmiao are among those exhibited. Fri 11–Sept 5.

③
'Hi, my name is Wayne. As a clairvoyant and master Tarot reader, I can help you in matters of the heart as well as questions about your life path. The journey to peace and love is right in front of you.'

Read more about Wayne
'It's all about finding your way. I've dedicated myself to making connections with each of my clients to ensure they get the best possible reading every time. And I'm proud to be able to prove to my clients time and again that my readings are fact-based, accurate and inspirational.'
Find out more. 10-minute psychic reading for only $10. Call 1-800-PSYCHIC

④

Capricorn (22nd December – 21st January) – the month ahead

Your sense of purpose is strong all month, thanks in part to the feeling of optimism that keeps you going from 1st through 10th. On the 3rd you find that all the seeds you have sown are beginning to flower, while on the 5th and 6th you realise that you are in control of your destiny. By the 11th you should be keeping a record of all that you've done, because time has a way of changing our memories. Do practical things on the weekend of the 12th instead of letting the desire for adventure take over. The 14th and 15th of the month will be very social, although you should keep an eye on your spending. If you're not careful, the 17th will find you broke and with a bunch of freeloaders. Be kind to these people at least through the 22nd. They're not trying to be mean and they really like hanging out with you. On the 24th you're ready for some real action. You'll step right into it without even noticing. Resist the impulse that you might feel on the weekend of the 26th to make big changes. You're back in control on the 28th, and that's where you'll stay.

⑤

Nostradamus, His Works and Prophecies
by Michel Nostradamus, Theodore Garencieres

EDITORIAL REVIEWS

About the author
Nostradamus (1503–1566) was a medieval physician who became an astrologer and prophet. His renown has grown immensely in recent years as we have witnessed the passing of his predictions. He wrote his prognostications in poetic form and they have challenged and inspired readers for over 400 years.

Book description
Has Nostradamus predicted the coming Apocalypse along with a thousand other great events? His believers claim that in the 1500s he predicted historic milestones that have or will alter the course of human history, such as the rise of Napoleon and Hitler. Published here are the hard-to-find original English translations from 1672 to help you answer that question. Finally, you can look through the actual work of Nostradamus to see if you can solve his riddles. Study of his work can be a fascinating hobby or intellectual exercise that can be quite enjoyable. What great event will be discovered next in this cryptic text?

⑥

Detailed Local Forecast for London, ENG

Tonight: Mostly cloudy. Low near 60F. Winds WSW at 5 to 10 mph.

Tomorrow: Partly to mostly cloudy. High 73F. Winds SW at 10 to 15 mph.

Tomorrow night: Clear to partly cloudy. Low 58F. Winds WSW at 10 to 15 mph.

Friday: Times of sun and clouds. Highs in the low 70s and lows in the mid 50s.

Saturday: Showers. Highs in the upper 60s and lows in the mid 50s.

Sunday: Mostly cloudy. Highs in the mid 70s and lows in the mid 50s.

2 **Which one of these sources (*1–6*, pages 39–40) might you consult if:**

a ... you were going on holiday to London?   [ ]

b ... you were a fan of art looking for something to do on
  a rainy day?   [ ]

c ... your birthday was in late December?   [ ]

d ... you were interested in the connection between history
  and the future?   [ ]

e ... you wanted to find out about the newest computer
  developments?   [ ]

f ... you wanted to find out about what is going to happen
  in your future?   [ ]

3 **Who or what is:**

a ... WorldExpo?

b ... Andy Warhol?

c ... Liu Zheng?

d ... a tarot reader?

e ... a psychic reading?

f ... a freeloader?

g ... Nostradamus?

h ... the Apocalypse?

i ... in the upper 60s?

4 **What do these words and abbreviations from the texts on pages
39 and 40 mean?**

a IT

b e-entertainment, e-marketing

c Tue–Sun

d avant-garde

e clairvoyant

f hanging out with you

g prognostications

h WSW

i mph

j 73F

C Using notes to help you write

1 What will life be like in the year 2050? Look at this student's notes on different aspects of the future. Use her notes to write her introductory paragraph about a day in her life in 2050.

Home	Technology	Food
• living on Mars • people – live forever • scientists – discover a way for people to live forever	• a robot – bring me coffee and breakfast in bed • talk to friends on Earth /Moon on telepathy phone	• food – dehydrated / in pills • nothing will grow on Mars

Compare your paragraph with the one in the answer key on page 106.

....

....

....

....

....

....

....

....

2   Read these notes and add your own ideas about life in the year 2050.

Technology Super computers that can speak to humans	**Science and medicine** A cure for AIDS
Work People will work at home by computer	**School** All learning will be done online with virtual teachers
Transport Cars will look different – run on other fuels	**Clothing** Special types of fabric
Entertainment Through the computer – virtual games	**Problems** Overpopulation

3   Use your notes to write about a day in your life in the year 2050.
     Include the following information.

a general life circumstances
b getting up in the morning
c your daily routine
d the end of the day

....
....
....
....
....
....
....
....
....
....
....
....
....

UNIT 7

The effect of colour

1 Read the following sentences. They each summarise one of the
paragraphs in the text *The pink police station*. What do you think
each paragraph will say?

a Choose an appropriate colour whatever you're doing.   [   ]
b Choosing room colours is important.   [   ]
c Colour and the nervous system.   [   ]
d Colour preferences reveal personality.   [   ]
e Good colour choices match eye colour.   [   ]

Read the text. Match the summaries with the correct paragraphs.

2 Read *The pink police station* again and then tick the best answers.

a The energy of a particular colour:
  1 ... makes us feel fed up.   [   ]
  2 ... attracts us to the colour.   [   ]
  3 ... always expands our cells.   [   ]

b People are attracted to colour therapy because:
  1 ... they are disillusioned with their lives.   [   ]
  2 ... they've lost confidence in normal doctors.   [   ]
  3 ... their doctors say colour is good for them.   [   ]

c Max Luscher's test:
  1 ... is now only used by psychologists in Switzerland.   [   ]
  2 ... reveals the sequence in which governments use
      the Internet.   [   ]
  3 ... is designed to show what kind of a person you are. [   ]

d Interior designers make mistakes because they:
  1 ... don't consider what kind of people they are designing
      for.   [   ]
  2 ... understand why they should paint dining rooms blue. [   ]
  3 ... are convinced by the theory that pink calms people
      down.   [   ]

e The best clothes colours:
  1 ... are hazel and green if your eyes are blue.   [   ]
  2 ... go with the colour of the wearer's eyes.   [   ]
  3 ... are shades of red that the wearer likes.   [   ]

THE PINK POLICE STATION

If colour is energy, is blue right for the dining room?

1 Now here's a theory: you and I are energy. We are colour. When we're feeling fed up and run-down, this may mean that we have too much or too little colour in us. Each of us is inadvertently attracted to one colour more than others, and the reason for this is that colours have energy in them, and that is what draws us to them. Every colour affects our cell structures, sending very fine chemical vibrations on to our nervous system, which via the pituitary gland directs our body. For instance, blue light makes our cells expand but red light makes them contract. Each colour in the spectrum, in other words, has its own special effect on us and as we absorb its energy it travels via the nervous system to the part of the body that needs it. And so, as people look for alternatives to mainstream conventional medicine, which they think is unsatisfactory, and seek new ways of making themselves well, they – we – have turned to colour therapy as a new way of chilling out, a way of restoring our individual states of optimum well-being and restoring an appropriate physical and mental balance.

2 You think that sounds too extreme? Well, according to the Swiss psychologist Max Luscher, colour and personality are so closely linked that he developed a test to reveal character traits by the sequence in which a subject chooses colours. The test is now used by psychologists and governments across the world – and a version of it even appears on the Internet for anyone to use.

3 Top colour therapist Angela Wright agrees that colour elicits a strong psychological response – which is why the appearance of rooms in a house is so vital to its inhabitants' well-being. 'The biggest mistake interior designers make is not to take into account the personality of the client whose home they are decorating and the activity associated with a particular room', she says. For instance, if you painted your dining room blue, then, says Wright, 'you'd have very boring dinner parties because that colour is calming. As a result, everyone would be on their best behaviour'. One police force in southern

Britain was so convinced by theories of colour that they painted their cells pink – a nurturing, romantic colour – to try and stop their temporary guests feeling aggressive.

4 According to fashion expert 'Annie', a columnist for Britain's *Observer* newspaper, certain colours suit people better than others, and so care should be taken when selecting clothes. There's nothing new about that of course. People with good dress sense have always worried about what to wear, and colours go in and out of fashion. But Annie goes further than this. She suggests that the best colours are those that complement or reflect the wearer's eye colour. If you have hazel eyes, for example, certain shades of green are just right. However, in what seems like a contradictory point of view, she is adamant that people should be allowed to wear whatever colours they feel good about, even if they are not appropriate: 'I know people who don't really suit red, for example,' she wrote in a recent column, 'yet derive enormous pleasure from wearing it, and who has the right to tell them otherwise?' Well, no one has the right, but perhaps it would be kind!

5 So there it is. Colour counts, and it's important for all of us. If the kitchen needs repainting, or if you're thinking of having the living room done; if you feel like having your hair dyed or you just want to go out and spend money on clothes, work out what colour suits your personality and your looks best: learn which ones will affect your nervous system and how they will do this. Take colour seriously and it will improve your life – and make you feel good about it too.

3 Which of the words highlighted in blue in the text on page 45 means the following?

a get ....
b gets something from someone ....
c look good with ....
d looking after, caring for ....
e ordinary ....
f relaxing completely ....
g small shaking movements ....
h the opposite of *expand* ....
i very sure ....
j without meaning to ....

Language in chunks

4 What do the following phrases from the text *The pink police station* mean?

a has its own special effect on us (paragraph 1)

....

b seek new ways of (paragraph 1)

....

c elicits a strong psychological response (paragraph 3)

....

d on their best behaviour (paragraph 3)

....

e has the right to (paragraph 4)

....

5 Re-write the following sentences using the phrases in blue.

a I don't like brilliant sunshine.   has a bad effect

....

b Interior designers want to combine colours.   seeking new ways of

....

c The colour red seems to make bulls react.   elicits a strong psychological response

....

d When their grandmother comes to tea, the children are always good.   on their best behaviour

....

e No one can order me about. I'm a free agent.   has the right to

....

B Six thinking hats

Edward de Bono is regarded as the leading international authority in conceptual and creative thinking and in the teaching of thinking as a skill. He originated the term 'lateral thinking', which now has an entry in the Oxford English Dictionary, and is well known for the deliberate creative techniques associated with it and for the powerful 'six thinking hats' method.

1 a Do you know this man and anything about why he is famous? Read the introduction and find out.

   b What types of meetings do you attend? (For example: work, family, friends, clubs, class / school.) Make notes about some of the problems that happen at meetings.

   ....

   ....

   ....

   ....

   ....

   ....

2 Read the first part of the following passage quickly and answer these questions.

   a What do the six hats represent?

   ....

   ....

   b Why do people use the technique?

   ....

   ....

MAKING DISCUSSIONS AND MEETINGS MORE EFFECTIVE

Do you find meetings boring? Here's a technique that may help you.

In the 1980s, Dr Edward de Bono, a world-famous professor from Malta, invented a technique for group problem-solving called the 'six thinking hats'. Many large companies around the world, including IBM, Federal Express, British Airways and PepsiCo, have used this method to help them. But it would be just as useful for a school meeting or any other kind of group session.

The idea is that the whole group wears six different 'hats' when considering a problem. Each of these hats is given a different colour and represents a different way of talking and thinking about something.

There are three main reasons to use this technique.

- It focuses on the topic or problem, not on individual people.
- It allows people to look at the problem in many different ways.
- It allows people to all think effectively about a problem at the same time.

3 **Can you predict what the six different ways of thinking about a problem might be?**

Below is a summary of the different 'hats', what they signify and how the technique can be used. It is important that everyone in the group is thinking with the same hat at the same time. Imagine you are in a group trying to decide where to go on vacation together – here's how the six hats can help you.

When the group is thinking about facts and information, this is 'white hat thinking'. Here, you would think about how much money and time you have available, for example.

The red hat covers intuition, feelings and emotions. It allows the thinker to put forward an intuition without any need to justify it. 'Putting on my red hat, I think this is a terrible proposal.' Feelings and intuition can only be introduced into a discussion if they are supported by logic. Usually the feeling is genuine but the logic is spurious. The red hat gives full permission to a thinker to put forward his or her feelings on the subject at the moment. Red hat thinking is about emotions, thoughts and feelings. When the group puts on this hat, they respond to ideas emotionally, not logically. Here, people would discuss how they *feel* about the different places proposed.

The logical thinking hat, which calls for caution and careful analysis, is the black hat. This is the hat of judgement and caution. It is a most valuable hat. It is not in any sense an inferior or negative hat. The black hat is used to point out why a suggestion does not fit the facts, the available experience, the system in use, or the policy that is being followed. The black hat must always be logical. If someone suggests staying in a luxury hotel and there is not enough money, when you are wearing the black hat, you can discuss this. This is the logical positive hat and is used when discussing why something will work and why it will offer benefits. It can be used in looking forward to the results of some proposed action, but can also be used to find something of value in what has already happened.

The yellow thinking hat is the voice of positive reason. The group is looking for the benefits of suggestions and proposals. This is when the group would look at the advantages of the different places suggested.

The green hat is the hat of creativity, alternatives, proposals, things that are interesting and exciting changes. Creativity is called for when the group is wearing the green hat. Here, people would generate ideas for different places to go, combining ideas and thinking creatively.

The blue hat is the 'overview' or process control hat. It looks not at the subject itself but at the 'thinking' about the subject. 'Putting on my blue hat, I feel we should do some more green hat thinking at this point.' In technical terms, the blue hat is concerned with metacognition. The blue hat is the hat that makes an evaluation of the whole process of thinking. For example, if all the suggestions are in other countries and not everyone has a passport, someone might say, 'We need some more black hat thinking here'. If there is only one suggestion, you may need more green hat thinking.

Would you like your meetings and decision-making to be more creative, more positive and more logical? Would you like to have the opportunity to express your emotions without worrying? Why not give the 'six hats' idea of Edward de Bono a try? At the very least, it should make your meetings more fun!

4 Read the second part of the text (starting 'Below is a summary ...'). Complete the table about the six thinking hats.

Colour of hat	What are you thinking about when you wear this hat?

5 Can you guess the meaning from the context? Match these words from the text with their definitions.

a intuition   1 careful consideration of dangers ....

b spurious   2 knowledge of how you think ....

c caution   3 false, not real ....

d logical   4 broad, comprehensive investigation ....

e policy   5 using rational thinking ....

f overview   6 plan or system of action ....

g inferior   7 something you feel to be true, without knowing why ....

h metacognition   8 not as good as others ....

C Comparing and contrasting

1 Read this comparison of logical thinking and lateral thinking. Complete the table of characteristics based on the comparison.

Logical thinking calls for problems to be solved using the facts and evidence you have. You must follow a series of logical steps to work out the answer. It assumes that there is a 'right' answer and that by examining the facts and evidence carefully, you will arrive at this 'right' answer.

Like logical thinking, lateral thinking can also be very effective. But, on the other hand, lateral thinking asks you to 'think outside the box' and look for original, creative solutions to problems. The idea is to think in different directions, and to come up with answers that are not necessarily logical. Unlike logical thinking, it assumes that the logical answer is not always the appropriate answer or that there is not just one 'right' answer.

....
Logical thinking
Problem solved by **a** ....

The process: **b** ....
....
....
Assumes there is **c** ....
....
Lateral thinking
Problem solved by **d** ....

The process: **e** ....
....
....
Assumes there is **f** ....
....
....

2 Look at these words used for comparing and contrasting. Use the expressions in brackets to change the sentences below so that the meaning stays the same.

Contrasting	Pointing out similarities
however	both
compared to	similarly
on the other hand	likewise
nevertheless	too
while	like
whereas	also
unlike	

a Some people think colours have an effect on our mood, but not everyone believes this to be true.
  1 (however)..
  2 (nevertheless) ....
b The best colour for a person with blue eyes to wear is blue, and the best colour for someone with green eyes to wear is green.
  1 (while)..
  2 (whereas) ....
  3 (compared to)...
c People with green eyes and people with hazel eyes can wear shades of green.
  1 (both) ....
  2 (too)...
d A Luscher test can be taken online as well as in person.
  1 (likewise)..
  2 (similarly) ....

3 Read the comparison in Activity 1 again. Re-write the sentences with the words in blue, using expressions in Activity 2 instead of those words and keeping the meaning the same.

....

....

....

....

....

....

4 Write a comparison of left-brain dominant and right-brain dominant people using this table of characteristics.

- Write two paragraphs.
- Use some of the comparing and contrasting words from Activity 2.

Left-brain dominant people	Right-brain dominant people
* intellectual, use logic	* intuitive, use feelings
* remember names	* remember faces
* tend to use language in thinking	* tend to use images in thinking
* tendency to control their feelings	* tendency to be more free with their feelings

....

....

....

....

....

....

....

....

....

....

....

....

....

....

•••A What we eat

1 Read the short extracts (*1–4*) from different websites and match the extract to the website (*a–d*) it came from.

a www.mercola.com
the website of a medical doctor who specialises in nutrition and natural remedies ....

b www.monsantoafrica.com
a company which produces genetically modified (GM) crops ....

c www.greenpeace.org
an organisation in favour of protecting the environment ....

d www.vegan.org
a website dedicated to the arguments and health of people who don't use or eat animals ....

2 Who believes these things? Write *V* (vegans), *G* (Greenpeace), *Dr* (Dr Mercola) or *M* (Monsanto)?

a Humans need to eat some animal products. ....

b Humans do not have to eat meat. ....

c Genetically modified food is bad for us. ....

d Genetic engineering could feed the world. ....

e Vegetarian diets can be more healthy than meat-based ones. ....

f Genetic engineering is not a new thing. ....

g We do not know what the effects of GM food on humans are. ....

Which of these statements do you agree and disagree with?

What is a vegan? A vegan (pronounced VEE-gun) is someone who avoids using or consuming animal products. While vegetarians avoid flesh foods, vegans also avoid dairy products and eggs, as well as fur, leather, wool, feathers and cosmetics or chemical products tested on animals.

Why vegan? Veganism, the natural extension of vegetarianism, is an integral component of a cruelty-free lifestyle. Living vegan provides numerous benefits to animals' lives, to the environment and to our own health – through a healthy diet and lifestyle.

The consumption of animal fats and proteins has been linked to heart disease, colon and lung cancer, osteoporosis, diabetes, kidney disease, hypertension, obesity and a number of other debilitating conditions. Cows' milk contains ideal amounts of fat and protein for young calves, but far too much for humans. And eggs are higher in cholesterol than any other food, making them a leading contributor to cardiovascular disease. The American Dietetic Association reports that vegetarian / vegan diets are associated with reduced risks for all of these conditions.

Genetic engineering of food is a risky process. Current understanding of genetics is extremely limited and scientists do not know the long-term effects of releasing these unpredictable foods into our environment and our diets. Yet, GE ingredients are freely entering our food without sufficient regulations and without the consent and knowledge of the consumer.

Although transnational companies and their political supporters want us to believe that this food is safe and thoroughly tested, growing awareness of the dangers from GE food has started a global wave of rejection by consumers, farmers and food companies in many of the world's largest food markets. Due to consumer pressure, supermarkets have taken GE food from their shelves, global food companies have removed GE ingredients from their products and leading pig and poultry producers have promised not to feed animals with GE feed.

Along with the saturated fat and cholesterol scares of the past several decades has come the notion that vegetarianism is a healthier dietary option for people. It seems as if every health expert and government health agency is urging people to eat fewer animal products and consume more vegetables, grains, fruits and legumes. Along with this advice have come assertions and studies supposedly proving that vegetarianism is healthier for people and that meat consumption causes sickness and death. Several medical authorities, however, have questioned this data, but their objections have been largely ignored.

Many of the vegetarian claims cannot be substantiated and some are simply false and dangerous. There are benefits to vegetarian diets for certain health conditions and some people function better on less fat and protein, but, as a practitioner who has dealt with several former vegans (total vegetarians), I know full well the dangerous effects of a diet devoid of healthful animal products.

What has come to be called 'biotechnology' and the genetic manipulation of agricultural products is nothing new. Indeed, it may be one of the oldest human activities. For thousands of years, from the time human communities began to settle in one place, cultivate crops and farm the land, humans have manipulated the genetic nature of the crops and animals they raise. Crops have been bred to improve yields, enhance taste and extend the growing season.

Each of the 15 major crop plants, which provide 90 percent of the globe's food and energy intake, has been extensively manipulated and modified over the millennia by countless generations of farmers intent on producing crops in the most effective and efficient ways possible.

Today, biotechnology holds out promise for consumers seeking quality, safety and taste in their food choices; for farmers seeking new methods to improve their productivity and profitability; and for governments and non-governmental public advocates seeking to stave off global hunger, assure environmental quality, preserve bio-diversity and promote health and food safety.

3 Match the words (a–k) from extracts 1–4 on page 53 with their synonyms or definitions (1–11).

a numerous (extract 1)
b risky (extract 2)
c consent (extract 2)
d urging (extract 3)
e objections (extract 3)
f substantiated (extract 3)
g cultivate (extract 4)
h yields (extract 4)
i enhance (extract 4)
j millennia (extract 4)
k advocates (extract 4)

1 grow ....
2 thousands of years ....
3 proved ....
4 many, lots of ....
5 dangerous ....
6 trying to persuade, strongly advising ....
7 productivity, harvests ....
8 permission, agreement ....
9 expressions of disapproval ....
10 supporters ....
11 improve ....

Language in chunks

4 Complete the phrases (a–g) with as many of the words and phrases opposite – some of which come from the web extracts – as you can.

a a debilitating ....
b associated with ....
c global ....
d stave off ....
e intent on ....
f devoid of ....
g linked to ....

condition	protest	animal products
illness	destroying	vitamins
sickness	winning	dying earlier
disease	emotion	poverty
wave of rejection	producing	living longer
hunger	protein	
terrorism	fat	

5 Use one of the expressions you made in Activity 4 to complete these sentences as in the example.

a The United Nations got together to try to do something about the number of poor people in the world in a conference on _global poverty_ .

b He ate a diet which was .... , because he knew of the dangers of fat to his health.

c Exercising every day has been .... Experts say this can add five more years to your life.

d She was in a wheelchair, because of .... that she had had for 20 years.

e The football player was .... This was his last chance before he retired from the game.

f She ate a chocolate bar to .... , as she would not be eating dinner for at least another two hours.

g Obesity has often been .... , probably because of all the illnesses that it can cause.

●●B The battle of the diets

1 Read the four descriptions of different weight-loss systems (on page 56) and write the name of the system each person invented under the picture.

Dr Arthur Agatson

Dr Robert Atkins

Bernice Weston

Dr Barry Sears

....

2 Now read the passages again and answer these questions. Who or what:

a ... are bad carbs?   ....

b ... was overweight as a child?   ....

c ... believes in healthy eating?   ....

d ... wanted to improve his own health?   ....

e ... is only allowed to eat 20g of carbs a day? ....

f ... are natural carbohydrates?   ....

g ... gets weighed every week?   ....

h ... is or was a cardiologist?   ....

i ... are good fats?   ....

j ... called Dr Atkins an intriguing person?   ....

k ... thinks it's important to diet with other people? ....

l ... believes in a low-carb diet?   ....

Named one of *People* magazine's '25 most intriguing people' at the end of the 20th century and one of *Time* magazine's 'people who mattered' at the end of 2003, Dr Atkins was a cardiologist with a pioneering perspective on nutrition and health. The Atkins Diet suggests that conventional medicine's low-fat approach to dieting just isn't working. Instead, Dr Atkins and his followers advocate a high-protein, low-carbohydrate (low-carb) approach to losing weight. What makes the Atkins Diet so controversial is its two-week induction phase, which is the first stage of the programme. Dieters eat virtually no carbohydrates (only 20g per day from vegetables are permitted), but can eat fatty foods freely. This means absolutely NO bread, pasta, rice or fruit, but liberal amounts of meats (including red meat and bacon) and full-fat cheese.

· ·

The South Beach Diet is designed not only to help you lose weight but also to improve your health. It was developed by Dr Arthur Agatson. Agatson's idea is not that all carbs and fat are bad, but that we have to learn to eat only 'good' carbs such as those found in fruits and vegetables, and eliminate 'bad' carbs (those found in processed foods like breads, snacks and soft drinks). According to Agatson, our bodies cannot process these foods adequately and, as a result, the body stores more fat than it should, especially in the midsection.

The diet also allows plenty of healthy monounsaturated fats such as olive and canola oils as well as meats and seafood. These are the 'good' fats. In addition to actually reducing the risk of heart attack and stroke, they taste good and make food palatable. They're filling too.

· ·

In 1976, Brooklyn-born Bernice Weston founded Weight Watchers of Great Britain on a budget of £1500. In ten years, the organisation had grown to 800 clubs and 1.5 million members. Her story is an inspiration for the weight-loss system that she started. From being just a 'fat girl', she has become one of the most successful businesswomen of her generation.

Weight Watchers works by assigning points to foods according to how many calories they contain and allowing members to eat a certain amount of 'points' per day. The most important part of the Weight Watchers system is the weekly meetings where members go for their weigh-in and meet with other members as a kind of support group to encourage each other to continue with the diet in order to reach each individual's 'weight-loss goal'. The leaders of the meetings are all people who have lost weight themselves as members of Weight Watchers.

Dr Sears began the research that led to the development of the Zone Diet for a very selfish reason: he wanted to do what he could to support his heart. All the males on his father's side of the family had died of heart disease in their early 50s and he didn't want to be one of them.

Dr Sears thinks that Mother Nature has designed our digestive system to operate correctly when eating just two food groups: (1) lean protein like boneless, skinless chicken and (2) natural carbohydrates like fruits and fibre-rich vegetables. Sears feels that our bodies are not able to deal adequately with grains, bread and pasta as the digestive system was not designed to process these.

The Zone Diet works on the idea that every meal that we eat should contain 40 per cent of its calories from carbs, 30 per cent from protein and 30 per cent from fat (fat is found in meats, seafood, dairy products, nuts and even some fruits like avocados). Each person eats the amount of food she or he needs according to a chart based on weight and how active she or he is. Seven grams is known as one 'block' in this diet.

3 Read these lists of ingredients (*a–d*) and match them with the directions for making the recipe (*1–4*).

a ....

- 2 cups of broccoli, flower clusters, raw
- 3 ounces of boneless, skinless chicken breast, raw
- 2 teaspoons of olive oil, extra light flavour
- ¼ cup of black bean sauce
- 1 cup of orange segments

b ....

- 4 tablespoons extra virgin olive oil
- 1 garlic clove, crushed
- 3 boneless skinless chicken breast halves, cut into strips
- ⅛ teaspoon salt
- ¼ teaspoon coarsely ground black pepper
- ½ cup dry white wine
- 3 medium tomatoes, sliced

c ....

- medium chicken breast (2.5)
- medium portion of pasta (2)
- broccoli (0)
- pureed tomatoes (0.5)
- 10g half fat cheese, grated (0.5)
  (5.5 points per serving)

d ....

- 2 tablespoons olive oil, divided
- 1 small onion, chopped
- ½ small carrot, chopped
- 1 celery stalk, chopped
- 2 garlic cloves, sliced
- 2 ounces baked ham, diced
- 2 pounds boneless, skinless chicken thighs
- ½ cup red wine
- ½ cup reduced-sodium chicken broth
- ½ bay leaf
- 2 tablespoons chopped fresh parsley

1   Burgundy chicken

1. Heat 1 tablespoon oil in a large, heavy skillet over medium heat. Add onion, carrot and celery. Cook 5 minutes, until vegetables soften. Add garlic and ham and cook 2 minutes more. Transfer mixture to a bowl.
2. Heat remaining oil and brown chicken thighs. Add wine, broth and bay leaf to skillet. Reduce heat to medium-low and cook 35 minutes, until chicken is cooked through and most of the liquid is reduced. Return vegetables and ham to skillet. Mix well and heat through for 5 minutes. Sprinkle with parsley before serving.

2   Broccoli chicken with Chinese black bean sauce

Cut broccoli into bite-sized pieces. Cut chicken into bite-sized pieces. Heat oil in nonstick pan and toss in broccoli. Cook about one minute and add chicken pieces. Cook chicken and broccoli until chicken is done and broccoli is bright green. Add black bean sauce, stir and remove from heat.

Enjoy orange sections for dessert.

The recipe is 3.3 blocks, balanced, and only 315 calories!

3   Chicken in white wine

In a medium skillet, heat the oil and garlic over medium heat. Sprinkle the chicken with the salt and pepper, then add to the skillet and cook for 7 to 10 minutes. Add the white wine and cook for an additional 2 minutes.

Remove the chicken to a platter. Sauté the tomatoes in the skillet for 2–3 minutes. Place the tomatoes over the chicken and cover with the pan drippings.

4   Chicken, tomato and broccoli pasta

Dice and dry-fry chicken breast until cooked thoroughly.

Cook pasta and broccoli as normal.

Slowly heat the tomatoes in a pan for a few minutes or heat in microwave.

Mix chicken and drained broccoli into tomatoes and serve on a bed of pasta, topped with cheese.

4 Match the definitions (1–8) to the words (a–h), taken from the list of ingredients in Activity 3.

a stalk   1 with the skin removed ....
b clove   2 made into a powder ....
c chopped   3 stick ....
d crushed   4 made into a liquid or paste ....
e ground   5 cut into small pieces ....
f boneless   6 with the bones removed ....
g skinless   7 pressed until broken ....
h pureed   8 small section of a bulb of garlic ....

5 Read the recipes on page 57 again and match the type of diet with the recipe.

a Burgundy chicken   1 Weight Watchers ....
b Chicken in white wine   2 the Zone Diet ....
c Chicken, tomato and broccoli pasta   3 the Atkins Diet ....
d Broccoli chicken with Chinese black bean sauce   4 the South Beach Diet ....

6 Match the meaning of the words (a–h) with the definitions (1–8).

a skillet   1 the fat and juices from meat ....
b sprinkle   2 partly covered ....
c sauté   3 with the liquid removed ....
d drippings   4 cook lightly in oil, turning constantly ....
e dice   5 pan used for frying ....
f fry   6 scatter or release in small drops or particles ....
g drained   7 cook in oil ....
h topped   8 chop into small pieces ....

•• C Describing graphs and tables

1 Read the report about this table and identify these three parts of the report.

a conclusions which are based on the table ....
b description of what the table represents ....
c description of the information in the table ....

Table 1: *1203 people in the UK were asked whether they would eat food which contained GM ingredients.*

1	If you knew which food had GM ingredients and you could choose, which of these is your opinion?	
	I would never eat GM food.	42%
	I would prefer not to eat GM food.	51%
	I don't mind whether or not I eat GM food.	7%
	I would prefer to eat GM food.	0%
	I would always eat GM food.	0%

Report on Table 1

Part 1
This table shows the results of a survey carried out in the UK, in which 1203 people were asked whether they would eat food which contained GM ingredients.

Part 2
The results show that 42 per cent of the people asked would never eat GM food if they knew that it had GM ingredients, while about half (51 per cent) said they would prefer not to eat GM food. Seven per cent of the people surveyed said they don't mind whether or not they eat GM food and no one said they would prefer to eat GM food or would always eat GM food.

Part 3
This seems to show that people in the UK do not like GM food and do not want to eat it if they have a choice.

2 Now look at Table 2. Write a report on what the table shows, using the plan below.

Table 2: *Two hundred people were asked the following question by Australian High School students: 'In your opinion, are the dangers of genetic modification of plants more important than the possible advantages?'*

Part 1
This table shows ...

Part 2
The results show that ...

Part 3
This seems to show that ...

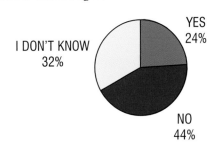

YES 24%

I DON'T KNOW 32%

NO 44%

●●A On beauty and hair

1 Complete the table in note form with opinions from the text on page 61.

Advantages of being a blonde woman	Disadvantages of being a blonde woman

2 Read the text again. Who or what:

a ... make their hair lighter in some way?

....

b ... was discovered nearly 200 years ago?

....

c ... says that fair-haired, fair-skinned people are more attractive?

....

d ... found out that being a blonde woman is bad for your job prospects?

....

e ... gets better pay?

....

f ... makes you look younger?

....

g ... said that hair colour had not affected them?

....

h ... gave brunettes more money?

....

i ... thinks brunettes are cleverer and more capable than blondes?

....

THE NEW BLONDE BOMBSHELL

Do blondes have more fun? Women certainly assume so, for while only one in six is a natural blonde, almost half of all women lighten their hair in some way or another.

Peroxide was discovered in 1818. Two centuries on, most blondes get a little help from the bottle. Last year they spent over £100 million on hair dye – and that doesn't include what they pay at the hairdressers to help to emulate blonde role models such as Britney Spears, Sharon Stone and Gwyneth Paltrow.

In fact many of these golden-haired icons are not natural blondes either. Even Marilyn Monroe started out as a freckle-faced brunette with medium skin tone. She wore pale make-up and dyed her hair platinum. So what is the mystery magnet that draws women to becoming blonde? It must be strong, because even today across all races – not just white westerners – when people are asked to rate others for 'attractiveness', they usually opt for those with lighter hair and skin. You only have to check out the TV commercials around the world to see how important the image of the blonde has become.

Until recently, being blonde or brunette was reckoned to be merely a matter of fashion. But something much deeper is driving our reactions to hair colour. In fact, it turns out, being blonde, whether natural or 'fake', may not do women any good at all.

Recent research conducted by, among others, Diana Kayle at California State University reveals – amazingly – that while being blonde may boost your social life, it can also damage your career prospects. Blonde females are rejected for jobs more often than equally-qualified brunettes. And where blondes and brunettes are given similar jobs, the darker-haired applicants are awarded higher salaries. It seems hardly credible that such changeable features as hair colour could so influence recruitment decisions, but the research findings are unequivocal.

So what lies behind this remarkable bias? One theory is that blond hair gives the appearance of youth. This is because people have lighter hair and skin when they are children than when they get older. So blonde people are treated (unconsciously – we are not aware we are doing it) as if they were less intelligent, more naïve, more vulnerable, less mature and less capable.

Brian Bates did an experiment for a BBC television programme. Business students were given CVs for six job applicants. There were photos attached. Some of the candidates had brown hair, the others were blonde.

When they were asked whether the photos had affected their choices, the business students were convinced that hair colour had not influenced them. 'The picture, for me, didn't play a major part,' said one. 'I made a studious attempt to ignore the appearance of the applicants,' said another. 'I focused primarily on the CV,' insisted a third.

But the result revealed a different story. While they had appointed the blondes and the brunettes almost equally to the job, they had awarded the brunettes a higher salary.

Under close questioning, they revealed that the blonde stereotype had indeed affected their judgement. 'The woman with blonde hair is more of a wannabe – I would think she is probably an experienced secretary or something,' confessed one. 'She looks like a PA rather than a middle manager,' said another. 'The brunette does look more like one would imagine a middle manager would look.'

Men tend to rate blondes as more feminine but less intelligent than brunettes. Studies in Ireland confirmed that men rated blonde females as of significantly lower intelligence than brunettes and in America, job applicants were rated as less capable and assigned a lower salary than brunettes. In other words, blondes are seen as attractive, but dumb.

All blondes, but are they *real* blondes?

3 Complete the sentences with the following work-related words from the text on page 61.

| applicant |
| appointed |
| CV |
| equally qualified |
| PA |
| reject |
| salary |

a If you apply for a job, you are a job ....

b When you apply for a job, you generally send information about yourself, called a curriculum vitae or .... for short.

c Two people who have studied the same thing are ....

d If the interviewers don't give you the job, they .... you.

e If you are the successful candidate for the job, you are ....

f The amount of money you get paid per month is called your ....

g The manager's chief aide is his / her personal assistant (often a higher-status job than a secretary). This is often shortened to ....

Language in chunks

4 Read the extracts from the text on page 61. Re-write the sentences, replacing the phrases in blue with words or phrases which mean almost the same.

a Most blondes get a little help from the bottle.

....

b While being blonde may boost your social life, it can also damage your career prospects.

....

c It seems hardly credible that such changeable features as hair colour could so influence recruitment decisions.

....

d The picture, for me, didn't play a major part.

....

e I made a studious attempt to ignore the appearance of the applicants.

....

f Under close questioning, they revealed that the ... stereotype had ... affected their judgement.

....

B Beauty and sadness

1 Read the biographical note and complete the table.

Nick Drake (pictured), a British singer-songwriter, was born in 1948 and died in 1974. He made three records that everyone said were fantastic, but hardly anybody bought. But, since his death, his fame has grown, so that more than 30 years later, his songs have been included on the soundtrack of at least three Hollywood movies, and documentaries about him and his music have been aired repeatedly on American and British radio and television. The latest of these was a radio programme narrated by the Hollywood star Brad Pitt, a committed fan. Many 21st-century musicians (Coldplay, Beth Orton, Norah Jones, for example) say his music influenced theirs, and there are countless websites devoted to his memory and his music.

Name	a	
Dates	b	
Number of records	c	
Admirers of his music	d	1
		2
		3
		4

2 On page 64, read the comments which were sent to a recent BBC website about Nick Drake. Who:

a ... first heard Nick Drake's music in a documentary on American radio?

b ... first heard Nick Drake's music in a television commercial?

c ... first heard Nick Drake's music because of a friend from Scotland?

d ... first heard Nick Drake's music when her boyfriend played it to her?

e ... first heard Nick Drake's music when her father played her some of it?

f ... liked Nick Drake's music the moment he first heard it?

g ... once talked about the mixture of beauty and sadness in Nick Drake's music?

h ... only listens to Nick Drake's music at times that are very important for her?

i ... wants to tell everyone about Nick Drake's music?

I was introduced to Nick Drake's music by a Scottish pen-friend some 14 years ago at the tender age of 16. I don't think there is much else that I listened to and loved back then that I still listen to on a regular basis. Nick Drake's music is timeless and beautiful, melancholic yet uplifting – I always return to it.

Sarah Beatrice, Bristol

I first heard of Nick Drake on 'E' Network, which is a local cable station in my area. A documentary was aired a few years ago. It captured my attention instantly. There was this lovely, haunting beauty in his words and melodies that just sucked me into another dimension. I was obsessed with finding a CD. It was so different from anything I'd ever heard. It was like finding a lost treasure. I rarely hear of any fans mentioning how charming he looked as a man. I just can't find the words to describe how much Nick's music has captivated and enchanted me since the discovery and I never tire of listening.

Tonya Swift, Little Rock, Arkansas

I was introduced to Nick Drake's music just over a year ago and I was instantly captivated by it. His music is so incredibly beautiful and the words are so poignant. I particularly love 'Man in a shed' and 'Time of no reply' but I don't have one favourite song as they're all truly unique. His songs have inspired my music so much. I am glad his music is getting recognition as he deserves it. If only he could be here today to see the recognition he is now getting.

Bentley, Derbyshire

Nick's music was introduced to me by a now ex-boyfriend. I am extremely fortunate to have encountered his work, which I find is sometimes inspirational, sometimes haunting; it just hits the spot for 'mood music'.

Usha Jain, London

I'm almost embarrassed to say I found Nick Drake through a commercial for the Volkswagen Cabrio. 'Pink Moon' was the background music; it haunted me. I searched the Internet for mentions of the song and finally found Nick Drake. What a revelation!

Jesse, Glendale, California

My dad first introduced me to Nick Drake's work at a time in my life when I had lost my way a bit. The first song I heard was 'Way to blue' and ever since then, I've bought every one of his albums. At first, his music made me feel sad, but now I see his work as an inspiration to us all. I believe Nick's music helped me to recover from my problems and, although I am only 17, I have played his music to all my friends and they agree that there is something to be said about music that is not necessarily from our era but is still truly great. It is one of my missions in life to spread the word and keep the memory of Nick Drake alive.

Lucy Sparrow, Bath

"Most people think his music is as sad as his life was, but I think there is a glimpse of beauty in that sadness." These were the words of a friend of mine who introduced me to Nick Drake's music just last summer. The first song I ever listened to was 'Cello song', and I became completely entangled in his music. I do not listen to his albums very often though. I guess this is in part because I would like to save his music for very special moments. But I can see why my friend thought that there was still beauty in all that sadness. Nick Drake will always be one of my favourite musicians, one of the few who can give me a sense of being alive in a world that is real. In such a world, people are able to experience the whole spectrum of emotions in succession, without feeling ashamed for that.

Alejandra Valero, Mexico

3 Write the names of the five songs by Nick Drake mentioned by the comment writers.

a ....

b ....

c ....

d ....

e ....

4 Match the words in blue in the text with the following definitions.

a a noun meaning the opposite of 'foreground'

....

b a verb meaning 'to be attracted very strongly by something when it is drawn to your attention'

....

c a verb meaning 'to be caught in something as if by ropes or a net'

....

d an adjective meaning 'not belonging to any particular period of history'

....

e an adjective meaning 'sad'

....

f an adjective meaning 'sad and impossible to forget'

....

g an adjective describing something that gives you ideas about how to make your life better

....

h an adjective describing something that makes you feel happier and more positive about the future

....

i a noun which means 'aims'

....

●●●C Curriculum vitae

1 Read the following document and complete the tasks which follow.

CURRICULUM VITAE

Name: Neil Todd
Date of birth: 30 / 10 / 85
Address: 26 Kingston Drive, Camelthorpe,
Cornwall CT54 7RF

Schools / Colleges attended:
1996 – 2003   Parkridge Community College
1990 – 1996   Camelthorpe Primary School

Exams: 2003   'A' levels in History, Maths,
English Literature (waiting for the results)
2001   GCSEs
History (Grade B)
Geography (Grade A)
Maths (Grade A*)
Biology (Grade A)
Spanish (Grade B)
Music (Grade C)
English (Grade A)
Art (Grade A*)
Physics (Grade C)
Chemistry (Grade B)

Employment record (including holiday jobs):
2002 November – present:
part-time work at GAP clothing store
2002 March – September:
Saturday working at Sainsbury's supermarket
2001 July and August:
part-time working at McDonald's

Hobbies and interests:
I like listening to music and going out to clubs. I
play the guitar. I'm keen on football (I go to
Camelthorpe's matches when they play at home).

Additional information:
My experience at the GAP clothing store means I
know a lot about shops, so I would be just right for
the job at the Speedo Sports Store.

I am trying to get a job for six months so that I can
then travel to Latin America before I start
University next year.

References:
Mary Fischer   Paul Pritchard
Manager   Headteacher
GAP   Parkridge Community College
23 High Street   34 Park Street
Camelthorpe   Camelthorpe
CT54 6SG   CT54 5SG

True or *False*? Write T or F in the brackets.

a Neil was born in September.   [ ]
b When he lists things in chronological order, the most
   recent thing comes first and the oldest thing comes last.   [ ]
c Neil has three 'A' levels (exams taken usually at about
   18 years old).   [ ]
d Neil's worst subject is history.   [ ]
e Neil has 11 GCSEs (exams taken usually at about
   16 years old).   [ ]
f Neil works for a department store.   [ ]
g Neil worked for the Next clothing store for eight months.   [ ]
h For a few months, Neil worked in a supermarket on
   Saturdays.   [ ]
i Neil worked for a hamburger restaurant full-time.   [ ]
j Neil plays the piano.   [ ]
k Neil follows his team to 'away' matches.   [ ]
l A teacher and an employer have agreed to write good
   things about Neil if they are asked.   [ ]

2 **Read the information about Nigel Thomas and complete his CV in
   the same way as Neil's. Imagine you are Nigel.**

Nigel Thomas was born in 1975. From 1980 to 1986, he went to Camelthorpe Primary school, and then, until 1993, he attended Parkridge Community College. A year later, he went to Leeds University, graduating in 1997. Then he did two years at Camelthorpe College of Further Education.

Apart from his GCSEs, Nigel got an A grade for 'A' levels in history and art, and a B grade in his English Literature exam. He also has a diploma in journalism. At university, his degree was a Bachelor of Arts Honours degree in history (BA Hons). He got a 2:1, which is the second-best degree you can get after a first (1).

Nigel has had many jobs, most recently as a reporter (since 2001) for the *Daily Mirror* newspaper. Before that, he worked for four years for the *Camelthorpe Daily News*. From 1994, he worked (for four years) in the Christmas holidays sorting holiday mail. In July and August 2001, he worked at McDonald's, and he did a gap year* in Tanzania in 1993–1994.

Nigel is keen on football and supports Chelsea football team in London. He plays tennis and he's an amateur painter.

Nigel thinks his experience equips him perfectly for the job of features editor at the *Times* Newspaper. The work he has done for the *Daily Mirror* (see enclosed documents) is exactly the kind that the advertisement is aiming for. He thinks that colleagues at the *Daily Mirror* will say that he gets on well with people and enjoys the atmosphere of a busy working newspaper.

For references, he is giving Morgan Peters, the *Daily Mirror* editor, and Martha Galvin, editor of the *Camelthorpe Daily News*.

* Students often take 'gap' years between school and university, or just after they finish university. They go and work as volunteers, usually abroad, or travel round the world as cheaply as they can.

Name:	Nigel Thomas
Date of birth:	a ....
Address:	26 Landsdowne Road, London SE3 4LR

Schools / Colleges attended:

b ....

c ....

d ....

e ....

Exams:

1993 'A' levels in

f ....

g ....

h ....

1991 GCSEs in
Maths (Grade A)
History (Grade A)
Maths (Grade A*)
Biology (Grade A)
French (Grade A)
Music (Grade A*)
English (Grade A)
Art (Grade A*)
Physics (Grade A*)
Chemistry (Grade A*)

Qualifications:

i ....

BA (Hons) j ....

**Employment record
(including holiday jobs):**

k ....

l ....

m ....

n ....

o ....

Hobbies and interests:

p ....

....

....

Additional information:

q ....

....

....

References:

r ....   Martha Galvin
Editor   Editor
Daily Mirror   s ....
36 Farringdon Street   1 High Street,
London EC4 2GY   Camelthorpe CT54 5SG

●●A *The Storm*

1 Read the text on page 70 and put the following events in the correct order. Number 1 is done for you.

a Eleanor went downstairs. ....

b Eleanor's sons and another man played cards. ....

c Francis thought pasta was the answer. ....

d Francis arrived home. ....

e Francis pushed the car. ....

f Francis put some music on. ....

g It stopped raining. ....

h Larry and Dean collected boxes of pasta. ....

i People from the office came back to the house because they hadn't been able to get home. ....

j Sofia caught some frogs. ....

k The music started again. ....

l Water began to get into the house. ...1... ◖║▬

Note: *Cannes* is a place in France where an annual film festival is held. *La Bohème* is an opera.

2 Did Eleanor enjoy the evening? How do you know?

....

....

....

....

.... ◖║▬

3 Match these definitions to the words in blue in the text.

a a loud noise in the sky ....

b a piece of meat that has been cooked in an oven

....

c a place where roads cross each other ....

d arranged as if in a theatre performance ....

e covered with water ....

f flowing quickly and in large amounts ....

g very wet ....

h walked slowly through water ....

i wonderful .... ◖║▬

Eleanor Coppola is the wife of the film director Francis Ford Coppola, and mother of Sofia Coppola who is also a film director. Many years ago, Eleanor went with Francis and their children Sofia, Roman and Giancarlo (Gio) to the Philippines where Francis was making one of his most famous films, *Apocalypse Now*. Eleanor wrote a diary of those days called *Notes*. The following extract describes an evening at the house they were renting.

The Storm

The storm got more exciting. Water started coming in the rooms downstairs. In some places the carpet looked like it was floating because there was a layer of water between it and the floor. The kids thought it looked like a water bed and were jumping on it. Pretty soon, the water was about six inches deep and it started out the bedroom door into the other rooms. Several people arrived from the office because the roads were so flooded they couldn't get home. It had taken them two hours just to get to our house. We were all in the kitchen opening bottles of Italian wine when someone realized that the boxes of pasta were sitting downstairs in the water. Larry and Dean took off their shoes and waded across the room, and started carrying the cartons upstairs. Francis finally arrived. He had been stuck at some flooded intersection for the past hour and a half. He had gotten out to push the car and was completely soaked. The editors had been at the house all day, preparing a reel of film for a screening at Cannes. They decided it was hopeless to try to make it home. So we began counting how many there were for dinner. There were 14, and the little half-eaten roast left over from lunch was about enough for four. Francis decided to make pasta.

Sofia put on her raincoat and was running around in the backyard. One section was under water and the frogs that usually hop around on the lawn there were all swimming. Sofia was chasing them and actually catching one now and then. The dirt from the flower beds was streaming into the swimming pool. Francis turned on *La Bohème* full volume. Marc, Roman and Gio were playing a noisy game of poker. The thunder and rain were so loud we were all shouting at each other. Finally, we did have a terrific dinner.

As we got to the dessert the electricity went off. We had bananas flambé by candlelight. After dinner, Francis and I were sitting on the couch looking toward the table. There were three candles and a group of people at each end of the long oval table. Francis was talking about how fabulous our eyes are that they can compensate for the low level of light and see perfectly clearly. You could never shoot in that amount of light. It was really beautiful. Francis was marvelling at how the people at the table were so perfectly staged. Now and then, someone would get up and go to the kitchen, crossing behind or in front of the light. Each person was so perfectly placed, leaning a little forward or a little back, catching the light, making shadows on the wall behind and silhouettes in front. He said you could never get it as good if you staged it. After a while we went to bed. I guess the rain stopped for a bit and everybody decided to try to go home.

They started out, they got to the main road and had to turn back.

The electricity came on at about four in the morning, and *La Bohème* started up, loud. The espresso machine began steaming, all the lights went on, and I went downstairs to shut things off. People were sleeping all over the place.

4 Answer the questions. Why:

a ... were the kids jumping on the carpet?

....

b ... did people arrive from the office?

....

c ... did Larry and Dean take off their shoes?

....

d ... was Francis very wet?

....

e ... did they cook pasta?

....

f ... was the swimming pool dirty?

....

g ... was everyone shouting at each other?

....

h ... did they eat by candlelight?

....

i ... are eyes better than cameras?

....

j ... did Eleanor get up in the middle of the night?

....

Language in chunks

5 Find the following phrases in the text *The Storm* and underline them.

a two examples of looked like
b a phrase which means *to succeed in getting back home*
c a phrase which means that someone *made* something *as loud as possible*
d a phrase which means *from time to time*
e an activity that took place by candlelight
f something that can compensate for something

●●● B Getting warmer

1 Look at these pictures from the movie *The Day After Tomorrow*. What is happening in the pictures? Did you see this movie when it came out, or have you seen it since?

2 Read the article from a San Francisco newspaper on page 73 and answer this question.

According to the author, why is global warming such an important problem?

....

....

....

....

....

....

....

....

....

....

....

....

3 Read these sentences. According to the article, which of them refer to the movie (*M*), which of them refer to real life (*RL*) and which refer to scientific predictions (*SP*)?

a Three hundred million people have to leave their homes because there are natural disasters. ....

b Global warming brings on a new ice age. ....

c There is a record level of carbon dioxide in the atmosphere. ....

d People in Europe do not have enough food to eat. ....

e Fewer than 20 per cent of people in the US know about the effects of cars on the environment. ....

f A million species of animals are in danger of extinction. ....

g There are more diseases that spread more quickly. ....

h Sea levels rise and flood cities that are near oceans. ....

i New York becomes frozen in ice very quickly. ....

j More than 40 per cent of the US population are not worried about global warming. ....

4 Choose and circle the word or phrase that could replace these words from the text so that the meaning stays the same.

a poised to
   1 about to very soon in the future
   2 never going to in the future
   3 going to in the distant future

b lethal
   1 harmless
   2 killer
   3 mild

c flee
   1 stay in
   2 escape from
   3 sell

d virulence
   1 weakness or gentleness
   2 quantity or amount
   3 strength or harmfulness

e influx
   1 flow
   2 escape
   3 dam

f swamp
   1 cover with ice
   2 cover with snow
   3 cover with water

g paradox
   1 contradiction
   2 possibility
   3 probability

h oblivious
   1 conscious
   2 unaware
   3 careful

i apathy
   1 lack of concern
   2 involvement
   3 strong feelings

CLIMATE CHANGE 'MORE DANGEROUS THAN TERRORISM'

It was, and still is, one scary movie. Thanks to global warming, in *The Day After Tomorrow*, the world literally freezes over. Yet how real was the science behind one of the decade's big disaster movies?

'Climate change is a far greater threat to the world than international terrorism,' says the science adviser to the British government. 'Temperatures are getting hotter, and they are getting hotter faster than at any time in the past,' says the international weather expert. 'Climate change is poised to change our pattern of life,' says an African ecologist. But successive governments in the US and elsewhere won't listen.

The number of extreme weather events has doubled from the decade before: lethal heatwaves in Europe, floods in Africa, droughts in Asia and the United States. A record 300 million people flee their homes from natural disasters. Carbon dioxide in the atmosphere hits record levels. Warming increases the range and virulence of diseases. Trees die in New England. Glaciers melt faster in Alaska. There's a major influx of freshwater in the North Atlantic and a slowdown of ocean circulation below the Arctic Circle. Antarctic ice flows faster into the ocean.

What could be next? Rising sea levels swamp coastal cities. Famine in Europe. Nuclear wars for water. A million species threatened with extinction. The end of life on Earth as we know it.

Sounds terrifying, but these aren't scenes from *The Day After Tomorrow*. They're from the real world. Everything in the second and third paragraphs has happened or is the statement of a real person (including Sir David King, chief science adviser to the British government). Everything in the fourth paragraph is science-based speculation.

The movie itself exaggerates the speed with which global warming brings on a new ice age, but the paradox that more heat might lead to more ice is real. If cold water from melting glaciers really does change ocean currents like the Gulf Stream, Manhattan could get colder pretty quickly – though in a decade, not a New York minute, as *The Day After Tomorrow* would have it. But all by itself, heat is already causing problems like drought, crop failures, disease, violent storms – and is threatening much more as the century proceeds.

Meanwhile, why haven't we noticed all this? Why are we determined to be oblivious? While 72 per cent of Americans said they were concerned about global warming in 2000, by 2004 this had gone down to 58 per cent and only 15 per cent believed it had anything to do with fossil fuel consumption. The combustion of fossil fuels (such as when you drive your car, or fly in a plane) produces carbon dioxide that contributes to the greenhouse effect and releases particles that are dangerous to breathe. Surely Mums and Dads, at least, should be worried about the effect on their children's health and their grandchildren's world? But perhaps it's hard to get upset about something that sounds so moderate and nice as 'global warming'? Even the 'greenhouse effect' sounds decidedly unthreatening. Who's afraid of a greenhouse?

Whatever the reason for our apathy, the climate crisis is the keystone issue of our time. Addressing it means addressing virtually every other significant environmental and energy problem and it must be done soon, because what is newest and most challenging about global warming is that once its effects are clearly apparent, it's too late to stop them.

●●● C Diaries

1 Read these diary entries. Which of the following (*a–d*) describes them best, do you think? Circle your answer and then look at the bottom of page 75.

The diary entries are written by:
a ... a bicycle thief who lives in Oxford.
b ... a fictional character (who wants to be a writer), and are meant to be funny.
c ... a Polish tourist, who is on holiday and goes sightseeing.
d ... a male model with a fear of dogs, who wants to find work in Oxford.

Monday April 15th
I was ten minutes late for work this morning. The exhaust pipe fell off the bus. Mr Brown was entirely unsympathetic. He said, 'You should get yourself a bicycle, Mole.' I pointed out that I have had three bicycles stolen in 18 months. I can no longer afford to supply the criminals of Oxford with ecologically-sound transport.
Brown snapped, 'Then *walk*, Mole. Get up earlier and *walk*.'

Friday May 24th
A house on my way to work has acquired an American pit bull terrier. On the surface, it seems to be a friendly dog. All it does is stand and grin through the fence. But in future I will take a different route to work. I cannot risk facial disfigurement. I would like the photograph on the back of my book to show my face as it is today, not terribly scarred. I know plastic surgeons can work miracles, but from now on I am taking no chances.

Saturday May 25TH
Oxford is full of sightseers riding on the top deck of the tourist buses and walking along the streets looking upwards. It is extremely annoying to us residents to be asked the way by foreigners every five minutes. Perhaps it is petty of me, but I quite enjoy sending them in the wrong direction.

2 Choose one of the dates and answer the questions about it.

Monday April 15th

a Who is Mr Brown?

....

b What is the writer's surname?

....

c Why doesn't the writer use a bicycle? ....

....

....

d Is the writer's comment about Oxford criminals serious, sarcastic or funny?

....

....

....

Friday May 24th

a Why has the diary writer changed his route from his house to his work?

....

....

....

b What is the animal like?

....

c What does the diary writer fear? ....

....

d What is the connection between the following: disfigurement, scar, plastic surgery?

....

....

....

....

Saturday May 25th

a Where does the diary writer live? ....

b What do the tourists do?

....

....

c What does the diary writer enjoy doing? ....

....

d Do you sympathise with his criticisms of foreigners?

....

....

....

3 Complete one of the following tasks.

a List four things you did yesterday and write them as a diary entry.

b Write a diary entry for yesterday in which you put four things that you would really like to have happened, but which did not actually happen.

c Choose a famous character (living or dead). Write a diary entry which the character might have written.

....

....

....

....

....

....

....

....

....

....

....

The diary entries are from the book *Adrian Mole: the Wilderness Years* by Sue Townsend. Townsend's book is the humorous diary of a fictional character who always has bad luck and has peculiar opinions about everything (and who dreams of being a famous writer).

1 Read the passage quickly. What are the four types of reality TV shows mentioned? Give one example of each one.

	a	b	c	d
Type of show	Shows that go into someone's home.			
Example				

2 Read Julie Marsfield's *Opinion* again. Are these statements *True* (T) or *False* (F)?

a Andy Warhol's quotation is about reality TV. [ ]

b Huge numbers of people watch reality TV. [ ]

c Reality TV shows are usually expensive to make. [ ]

d Ordinary people often want to be on reality TV. [ ]

e Producers sometimes lie to people who go on the shows. [ ]

f People never talk about their personal lives. [ ]

g People on dating shows are always nice to each other. [ ]

h Most people probably act 'unnaturally' on reality TV shows. [ ]

i After appearing on a reality TV show, some people become famous. [ ]

3 Explain the meaning of the following words as they appear in the text.

a commercialisation (paragraph 1) ....

b ratings (paragraph 2) ....

c star (paragraph 2) ....

d eager (paragraph 2) ....

e manufactured (paragraph 4) ....

f controversial (paragraph 5) ....

g desperate (paragraph 7) ....

h appearances (paragraph 8) ....

In this week's Opinion, *Julie Marsfield looks at the phenomenon of reality TV and asks:*

Why on earth do they do it?

In 1968 Andy Warhol said, 'In the future, everybody will be world-famous for 15 minutes.' He was referring to the commercialisation of all aspects of our lives. With the growth of reality TV, his prediction seems to be coming true.

Reality TV shows are becoming more and more popular in Britain, the USA and other parts of the world. You may not understand why, but the ratings for these shows are high and they are relatively cheap to produce as the makers of the shows don't have to pay actors – they often star ordinary people eager for fame and who will jump at any chance to achieve it. We'll tell you why later, but first, let's look at the different types of show that come under the heading of 'reality TV'.

Firstly there are shows that go into someone's home and life and follow them around – *The Osbournes* is a typical example. The people on these shows are often famous and unusual in some way. This isn't always the case, of course, and sometimes the cameras may follow an ordinary doctor around or look at an everyday family as they deal with their problems. We get to look at other people's lives and compare them with our own.

Next, there are reality shows manufactured for TV, where the producers of the show put people into some kind of unusual situation and see how they react. In *Joe Millionaire*, 20 women were flown to a castle in France where they had the chance to meet Evan Marriott, who they were told was a multi-millionaire. In fact, Evan was a construction worker. In *The Real World*, seven young strangers are put together in a house for four months and cameras follow them around; the audience gets to observe how they get along with each other as they gradually open up about who they are. By now, we're all familiar with shows like this.

Then, what about those reality shows about real life where the people who come on seem to have no limits about revealing all – about their private lives and anyone else's! *The Jerry Springer Show* is famous for its controversial subject matter and guests on the show often get into physical fights with each other. Then, there are real-life courtroom TV shows such as *Judge Judy* where people dispute a legal claim before millions of viewers. It seems that people on these shows will give very intimate details away and have no qualms about betraying their friends and family. Where do they find these people?

Last but not least, my own personal favourite, dating shows like *Elimidate* or *Blind Date*. On *Elimidate*, one person (either male or female) goes out on a date with four people of the opposite sex and, one by one, eliminates them until they finally choose the one person they would like to go on a 'real' date with. People criticise and humiliate each other (and themselves in the process) to 'win the competition'.

So, can someone tell me why these shows are so popular? Why do we love to see people doing desperate things for their '15 minutes of fame'? Is it that we see ourselves in these ordinary people? Or is it the opposite? Do we like to be reassured that we are normal and it's everyone else that's crazy? And anyway, do the people on these shows really act like this when the cameras are not following them around?

Well, maybe they're not crazy, nor are they even *trying* to act naturally. Do you remember the days when people appeared on TV because they were famous? Times have changed and now appearing on TV is a good way to *become* famous. Many people are using their appearances on a reality TV show as a step into show business, hoping that their careers will take off once they have been seen by millions of people. Think about it – do you know any 'celebrities' who started their career on a reality TV show? Reality TV gives people a chance to be noticed and when they appear on the show, they're hoping for far more than the 15 minutes that Andy Warhol promised!

See you next week.

Language in chunks

4   **Look at how these phrases are used in the text and then use them in the sentences which follow. You may have to change them a little to make them fit.**

with the growth of
jump at the chance
no limits about
to reveal all
no qualms about
one by one
to be reassured

a I don't want .... My private life should be private.

b He .... of being on the show. At last he was going to be famous.

c She has .... going by herself. She loves travelling alone.

d Do you have .... what you will do for money? How could you take that job?

e Jake's parents were worried about leaving him, but they .... by the fact that Lois was an experienced babysitter.

f .... the sales of DVD players, there are less VCRs being sold.

g They went into the room .... and sat down at their desks.

5   **Find these four multi-word verbs (a–d) in the text and match them to their meaning.**

a look at (paragraph 3)   1 have a good relationship with ....

b get along with (paragraph 4)   2 tell something that you're not supposed to tell ....

c give away (paragraph 5)   3 become popular ....

d take off (paragraph 8)   4 investigate ....

e Which of the verbs cannot be separated? ....

f Which verb cannot take an object? ....

g Which verb is followed by an adverb and a preposition? ....

h Which verb can stay together or can be separated? ....

6   **Use a form of the verbs a–d from Activity 5 to complete these sentences.**

a His new TV series has really .... It had the highest ratings this week.

b I don't .... my brother. We're very different.

c The detective was suspicious and decided to .... the relationship between the victim and her ex-husband more closely.

d Young children have a tendency to .... secrets very easily.

B What to watch

1 **Read the programme choices for Friday 28 May (on page 80).
Write the letters of the sentences in the correct rows.**

a It has people who nobody knows.
b It has six main characters.
c It has three finalists.
d It is difficult not to watch it.
e It puts a group of people into a house.
f It recreates scenes of how something was built.
g It's a programme where people sing in order to win.
h It's a 'situation comedy' (comedy series).
i It's about a historical figure.
j It's the first show in a new series of a popular reality programme.
k It's the last show in a long-running series.
l It's the last show of the third series.

Friends
Art of the garden
Big Brother: Live Launch Show
American Idol

2 **Read the *Today's Choices* page again. Who or what:**

a ... cried?
b ... designed the gardens of Blenheim Palace in 1760?
c ... have apparently chosen interesting people for their show?
d ... have big and powerful lungs?
e ... is an American version of a British TV show?
f ... is going to have their own new series?
g ... is in its fifth year?
h ... is married to a nice man?
i ... is sad and funny?
j ... tells a story about a garden designer or architect?
k ... was the owner of Blenheim Palace?
l ... wears informal / casual clothes?
m ... won the last series of *Big Brother*?
n ... buys and sells fish in the north of Scotland?

FRIDAY 28 MAY

TODAY'S CHOICES

SITCOM

Friends *9.00pm*

All right, I admit it, I cried. Quite a lot, actually, as the friends bid their last farewells after ten years – and this final show like all the others will be shown all over the world again and again and again! But even though it's the last show (and they are difficult to pull off), this one gets it just right. There are no great fireworks – this is a neat and, in some ways, quite a low-key tying-up of loose ends to make a highly satisfactory finale. It's sad of course, but it's frequently funny too, and there are some great jokes. Fans of the series would expect nothing less from a comedy that has been so good over such a long period of time.

So tonight we're joining the six as they start their new lives. Joey, of course, is the character who will live on in a new TV series. Chandler and Monica are preparing to become parents and move to the country, and Phoebe is married to sweet Mike. There's just the small matter of Ross and Rachel whose on-off romance has been such a big part of the show from the very beginning.

Rachel is heading off for a new life in Paris, while Ross is trying to work out where his future really lies. Everyone is very tearful – yes, they look like real tears – as Monica's apartment is packed up and they all leave it for the last time. So go on, get out those paper handkerchiefs. Just this once.

Alison Graham

GARDENING

Art of the garden *9.20pm BBC2*

Diarmuid Gavin tells the story of the designer Lancelot 'Capability' Brown, often called the nation's greatest landscape architect. In his scruffy jeans and cord jacket, Diarmuid takes us to Capability Brown's crowning achievement, the gardens of Blenheim Palace, surely one of Britain's greatest 'stately homes', and talks us through the story of their construction.

From 1760, thousands of labourers worked for years to dig a huge artificial lake, make a mile-long river and plant tens of thousands of trees.

The reason for all this hard work was to create a landscape that was totally beautiful and natural and which, more importantly, looked as if it had always been there. And it did. No one would have guessed how much effort it had taken if they hadn't known.

And how much money! The Duke of Blenheim, who owned the house, nearly went bankrupt paying for his gardens, and for years all he could see was a muddy field. Perhaps that's why he fell out with Capability Brown and started arguing with him – and why the programme makers feel they can have actors pretending to be the two men. Much better are reconstructions of the work in progress, and the programme has some incredible special effects that fool the eye into believing we are really there.

David Butcher

REALITY

Big Brother: Live Launch Show *10.00pm C4*

Love it or hate it, it's almost impossible to ignore *Big Brother*, which, like its ITV1 cousin *I'm a Celebrity ... Get Me Out of Here!* fascinates viewers and media alike for weeks. Even when the participants are as dull as ditchwater and the footage veers from mind-numbingly boring to downright infantile, the series pulls in big audiences. So, reluctant though you may be to get drawn into the experience, chances are you'll dip in at least once to see what all the fuss is about.

Now in its fifth year, the format remains unchanged (a group of unknowns move into the house for the summer, we watch their every move and vote one out every week until just the winner remains), although it's alleged that the makers have tried to recruit more exciting housemates this time. We'll just have to wait and see ...

Jane Rackham

MUSIC

American Idol *8.30pm ITV2*

Pop Idol's brash American cousin reaches the end of its third run. There are still three divas left in at press time but, assuming Jasmine Trias is voted out before the final, it'll be Fantasia Barrino, a wonderful soul singer, versus the contest's dark horse, the psychotically perky Diana DeGarmo. Both have lungs like traction engines, and are immune by now to any brickbats thrown by their harshest critic.

Jack Seale

TV Insider

We've got our eye on him

Whatever happened to Cameron Stuart, last year's winner of the fourth Big Brother series? Well, he's still involved in the fish trade on the island of Orkney, off the north-east coast of Scotland. But the 33-year-old has done a few extra things since his win. He's appeared in a pantomime in Aberdeen, he's writing a motoring column for his local paper and he's done some radio presenting for BBC Radio Scotland. 'I'm resolving to have as much fun this year as last year,' he says happily. But he's not planning on leaving his day job just yet. 'All the other things are just extras,' he says. 'But they're great!'

3 Complete the sentences with these words and phrases from the text.

a A rather literary way of writing that they say goodbye is

....

b When all of the story details are finally resolved, we talk of a

....

c A way of saying that something is not fantastically exciting or dramatic is ....

d Another way of saying 'he explains it' is to say 'he

.... it'.

e If there's a possibility that someone will win even if nobody expected them to, we can call them a ....

f If two people who once were friends disagreed about something, we can say that they .... each other.

g If we want to explain that a TV show is watched by a lot of people, we can say that it ....

h We often call sharp criticisms .... , especially when they are made about actors, singers, etc.

i When we are tricked by what we see, we say that it can

....

j When we don't know what's going to happen and we want people to know this fact, we can say that ....

k When we want to describe somebody's greatest success in their profession, we can talk about their ....

l A rather literary way of saying that something is very boring is to say that it is ....

as dull as ditchwater
bid their last farewells
brickbats
crowning achievement
dark horse
fell out with
fool the eye
pulls in big audiences
talks us through
there are no great fireworks
tying-up of loose ends
we'll just have to wait and see

●●●C Researching for writing

1   **Where do you usually get information when you need to write? Tick this list.**

I get information from:	often	sometimes	rarely	never
the Internet				
the library				
encyclopaedias				
a dictionary				
a grammar book				
textbooks				
asking other people				
magazines				
talking to an expert				
other sources				

Which resource is the most valuable for you? Which one is the least useful?

. . . .

2   **Look at this biography of Jackie Chan and complete Column *A* in the table (on page 83).**

Jackie Chan was born in Hong Kong in 1954. His real name is Chan Kong Sang. His parents were very poor – his father worked as a cook and his mother worked as a housekeeper in the French Embassy. Jackie hated school and left after primary school.

When he was seven, Jackie's parents enrolled him in the China Drama Academy and he often performed in public. Jackie Chan learned how to perform stunts at the academy, which he left when he was 17 to take up a career as a professional stuntman, appearing in Bruce Lee movies. Jackie's early career as an actor was not very successful and it was not until he added comedy to his action movies that he became very popular. Jackie Chan broke into Hollywood in the 1990s and is the biggest Hollywood movie star from Hong Kong. Today, Jackie Chan is famous all over the world with such movies as *Rush Hour 1, 2* and *3,* and *Around the World in 80 Days.*

Topics	A Information from the text	B Sequence number in the text
a Year of birth		
b His early career		
c How famous he is		
d What he learned in his studies (after school)		
e What he thought of school		
f What his position is today		
g What made him famous		
h Where he studied after school		
i Where he was born		
j Where he went to school		
k Who his parents were		

In what order is this information presented in the text? Write 1–11 in Column *B*. Why are things in this order?

3 Look at the chart about Shakira (Shakira Mebarak Ripoll). Where could you find more information about her?

Topics	Information
Date of birth	2 February 1977
Her early career	Started writing songs at eight years old. She signed a recording contract in 1990.
How famous she is	Famous worldwide with best-selling records in English, Spanish and Portuguese.
What she learned in her studies (after school)	
What she thought of school	
What her position is today	
What made her famous	Developed her own style of music, combining her Latin and Arabic influences with modern rock music.
Where she studied after school	
Where she was born	Barranquilla, Colombia
Where she went to school	
Who her parents were	Colombian mother, Lebanese father

Write a short biography of Shakira using the same sequence model as the text about Jackie Chan.

● ● ● A The blurb

1 The following is the blurb from the back of a book. Read it quickly. Identify the different parts of the page. Write the numbers of the different sections in the brackets.

a What other people have said about the book   [   ]
b Introduction to the book   [   ]
c What the book is about   [   ]
d Information about the author   [   ]

1 **From the acclaimed author of *High Fidelity* and *Fever Pitch* comes a great new novel about being a boy and becoming a man.**

2 **ABOUT A BOY**

Will is 36 and doesn't want children. He's selfish and self-centred and doesn't mind admitting it. Will thinks of himself as an island like Ibiza and he just wants to be left alone in his world without any responsibilities from the mainland. Thanks to his dad writing a song which is known all over the world, he has a great income and will never need to work a day in his life and he leads a life he loves. The last thing on his mind is settling down or getting married or doing anything as uncool as having a family. He just wants to live blissfully by himself in his cool apartment in London, where he has massive speakers and an awe-inspiring music collection. Is that too much to ask?

Marcus is 12 and he knows he's weird. He has a strange habit of singing for no reason – sometimes in the middle of maths class. This, unfortunately, makes him a figure of fun to the whole school. Marcus blames it all on his mother, who makes him listen to Joni Mitchell instead of Nirvana and read books instead of playing on his Gameboy. He loves his mum, but she is kind of different from everyone else's mum. She won't let him eat fast food or drink soda and she wears strange clothes – and makes Marcus wear them too.

Then Marcus meets Will and he recognises from a mile off that Will is cool. Marcus needs someone who knows what kind of trainers he should wear and who Kurt Cobain is. And Marcus's mother needs a husband. It all seems so perfect to Marcus ...

Hugh Grant and Nicholas Hoult in *About a Boy*

3 NICK HORNBY was born in 1957 and studied at Cambridge University. He is a former teacher and now lives and works in North London. He is the author of several novels and is also the pop music critic for *The New Yorker* magazine.

4 *"In his third novel, Hornby delivers another guaranteed bestseller – brilliant!"*
Books Today Magazine

"Hornby is one of the funniest contemporary writers ... Will is a character every man struggling to face up to his responsibilities will relate to."
The Sunday Review

2 Who:

a ... wrote a very famous song? ....

b ... wears unusual clothes? ....

c ... doesn't want to have children? ....

d ... tends to sing out loud? ....

e ... makes her son do things that are not cool? ....

f ... writes about pop music for a famous magazine? ....

g ... has a very large collection of music? ....

h ... wants someone to help him to be more cool? ....

3 Find these words in the text and explain what they mean.

a mainland ....   f former ....

b uncool ....   g delivers ....

c blissfully ....   h guaranteed ....

d massive ....   i struggling ....

e trainers ....

Language in chunks

4 Match these expressions from the text with a definition (1–7).

a to not mind admitting something   1 to accept ....

b to settle down   2 to start living a stable, secure life ....

c awe-inspiring   3 to be proud of, to not be ashamed of ....

d figure of fun   4 easily, without difficulty ....

e from a mile off   5 someone that people laugh at ....

f to face up to   6 to identify with, to understand ....

g to relate to   7 amazing, incredible ....

5 Now use the expressions in Activity 4 in the sentences below.
You may have to change them a little to make them fit.

a My daughter liked to go to parties all the time, but now she has .... and is married with two children.

b He finally had .... the fact that he was 30 years old and needed to get a job and earn some money.

c Janet could tell .... that this man did not want to have any responsibilities.

d She was sick of being a .... Why did no one take her seriously?

e The view from the top of the mountain was .... It was absolutely beautiful.

f She found the characters in the novel very difficult to .... as they lived in a different country and at a different time.

g It was his 50th birthday and he .... He knew he looked good for his age and he had made a great life for himself.

6   **Read the following two blurbs. Complete the table which follows in note form.**

With *Paula*, Allende has written a powerful autobiography whose acceptation of the magical and spiritual worlds will remind readers of her first book, *The House of the Spirits*.

Paula is a vivid memoir that captures the reader like a suspense novel. When the daughter of Isabel Allende, Paula, falls into a coma, the author begins telling the story of her family for her unconscious daughter. In the development of the story, there appear before us bizarre ancestors, we hear both delightful and bitter childhood memories, incredible anecdotes from her young years, the most intimate secrets passed along in whispers. In the background, Chile is ever present as we read about the turbulent history of the nation and her family's years of exile.

"Beautiful and moving ... it has everything and everything is marvellous."
Los Angeles Times Book Review

"Fascinating ... in a rich, impeccable prose, she shares with us her most intimate sentiments."
Washington Post Book World

Born in Peru, Isabel Allende was raised in Chile. She worked as a journalist for many years and only began writing fiction in 1981.

Now, for the first time, all six exciting parts of *The Green Mile* come together in one volume to let you enjoy Stephen King's gripping masterpiece.

At Cold Mountain Penitentiary, along the lonely stretch of cells known as the Green Mile, killers like the psychopathic 'Billy the Kid' Wharton and Eduard Delacroix await execution. Here guards as decent as Paul Edgecombe and as sadistic as Percy Wetmore watch over them. But good or evil, innocent or guilty, none have ever seen anything like the new prisoner, John Coffey. Is Coffey a devil in human form? Or is he a far, far different kind of being?

The truth emerges in shock waves in a way that will truly blow your mind.

"King surpasses our expectations, leaves us spellbound and hungry for the next twist of plot."
Boston Globe

"King's best in years ... A prison novel that's as haunting and touching as it is just plain haunted."
Entertainment Weekly

STEPHEN KING, the world's best-selling novelist, lives with his wife in Bangor, Maine.

	Paula	*The Green Mile*
Writer	a	e
Type of book	b	f
Brief description of contents / plot	c	g
Comments from reviewers	d	h

•• B From blurb to book

1 Read the three blurbs and then read the extract from *The Curious Incident of the Dog in the Night-Time* on page 89. Which is the correct blurb?

b *The Curious Incident of the Dog in the Night-Time* is a teenage romance unlike any other. The detective, and narrator, is 15-year-old Christopher Boone. Christopher has had a troubled childhood – made only bearable by a friendly policeman who lives at the end of his road. So when a neighbour's dog is killed, he is pleased to see his friend. But then things go wrong and Christopher gets into even more trouble as chief suspect in the dog-killing incident. Help comes from an unlikely quarter and the story of Christopher's friendship with Betty Shears, the neighbour's daughter, is a tale of loyalty, and finally love, which no reader will be able to resist.

a *The Curious Incident of the Dog in the Night-Time* is a science-fiction story unlike any other. The narrator is a 15-year-old robot-human, Christopher Boone. When Christopher finds a neighbour's dog murdered in the summer of 2217, the (cyber)police are called. Like all robot-humans, Christopher is keen on the police, but something goes wrong when he first meets the one assigned to the case. Christopher starts to investigate further, something robot-humans should not do under Galaxay code 57/6/53. But Christopher likes dogs, the last natural creatures on earth. His investigations take him deep into a galaxy-wide plot to change the universe, a journey that will challenge everything he has been programmed to think.

c *The Curious Incident of the Dog in the Night-Time* is a murder mystery unlike any other. The detective, and narrator, is 15-year-old Christopher Boone. Christopher has Asperger's, a form of autism, the mental condition that stops people from communicating with or understanding other people. He knows a lot about facts and maths, and very little about human beings. He loves lists, patterns and the truth. He hates the colours yellow and brown and being touched. He has never gone further than the end of the road on his own, but when he finds a neighbour's dog murdered, he sets out on a terrifying journey which will change his life for ever.

2 Read the extract again and circle the best answer in each case.

a The policeman thinks that Christopher is:
1 ... unlike normal 15-year olds.
2 ... older than most 15-year olds.
3 ... younger than most 15-year olds.

b The policewoman:
1 ... offers sympathy to the dog's owner.
2 ... arrests Mrs Shears.
3 ... goes to Mrs Shears' house to change her tights.

c Christopher becomes upset because:
1 ... the dog is dead.
2 ... the policeman is being nasty.
3 ... he can't deal with too many questions at once.

d Christopher mentions the bakery because:
1 ... he sometimes thinks of things getting crowded in his brain like bread in a bread slicer.
2 ... his Uncle Terry works there.
3 ... it has a bread slicer that is sometimes too slow.

e Christopher makes a noise which:
1 ... is like the white noise you hear on a radio.
2 ... he always makes when he can't cope with everything people are saying to him.
3 ... he always makes when he listens to the radio to make himself safe.

f The bakery and the radio are both:
1 ... things that really matter to Christopher.
2 ... things he uses to help us understand what is going on in his head.
3 ... things that his father and Uncle Terry worry about all the time.

g Christopher hits the policeman because:
1 ... he hates being touched.
2 ... the policeman thinks he killed the dog.
3 ... the policeman lifts him to his feet.

3 Find (a form of) these words and phrases in the text.

Now match the words and phrases with these explanations.

a a garden implement with three or four points ....

b a piece of clothing usually for women that covers the legs and goes up the waist ....

c a small cut on the skin ....

d to almost sit down, but without the bottom touching the ground ....

e I think I realise that. (sarcastic) ....

f to make a noise as if you are unhappy or in pain ....

g something that stops movement, usually in a small space ....

h to show a little bit (because some of it is still hidden inside or underneath something) ....

i to store in a pile ....

j to cut something into thin flat pieces ....

k to find a particular frequency on the radio when looking for a programme ....

l something found on trees ....

blockage
fork
to groan
I'd got that far.
leaf
to poke out
scratch
to slice
to squat
to stack up
tights
to tune

Extract from *The Curious Incident of the Dog in the Night-Time*

Then the police arrived. I like the police. They have uniforms and numbers and you know what they are meant to be doing. There was a policewoman and a policeman. The policewoman had a little hole in her tights on her left ankle and a red scratch in the middle of the hole. The policeman had a big orange leaf stuck to the bottom of his shoe which was poking out from one side.

The policewoman put her arm round Mrs Shears and led her back towards the house.

I lifted my head off the grass.

The policeman squatted down beside me and said, 'Would you like to tell me what's going on here, young man?'

I sat up and said, 'The dog is dead.'

'I'd got that far,' he said.

I said, 'I think someone killed the dog.'

'How old are you?' he asked.

I replied, 'I am 15 years and 3 months and 2 days.'

'And what, precisely, were you doing in the garden?' he asked.

'I was holding the dog,' I replied.

'And why were you holding the dog?' he asked.

This was a difficult question. It was something I wanted to do. I like dogs. It made me sad to see that the dog was dead.

I like policemen too, and I wanted to answer the question properly, but the policeman did not give me enough time to work out the correct answer.

'Why were you holding the dog?' he asked again.

'I like dogs,' I said.

'Did you kill the dog?' he asked.

I said, 'I did not kill the dog.'

'Is this your fork?' he asked.

I said, 'No.'

'You seem very upset about this,' he said.

He was asking too many questions and he was asking them too quickly. They were stacking up in my head like loaves in the factory where Uncle Terry works. The factory is a bakery and he operates the slicing machine. And sometimes the slicer is not working fast enough but the bread keeps coming and there is a blockage. I sometimes think of my mind as a machine, but not always as a bread-slicing machine. It makes it easier to explain to other people what is going on inside it.

The policeman said, 'I am going to ask you once again …'

I rolled onto the lawn and pressed my forehead to the ground again and made the noise that father calls groaning. I make this noise when there is too much information coming into my head from the outside world. It's like when you are upset and you hold the radio against your ear and you tune it halfway between two stations so that all you get is white noise and then you turn the volume right up so this is all you can hear and then you know you are safe because you cannot hear anything else.

The policeman took hold of my arm and lifted me onto my feet.

I didn't like him touching me like this.

And this is when I hit him.

C Book reports

1 Read these two book reports and complete the table with information about each one, as if you had written the book report.

Gandhi: A Life by Yogesh Chadha is a book about the life of Mahatma Gandhi, one of the key figures in the history of 20th-century India. It starts off with information about his life, such as where he came from and how he became a lawyer in the UK and South Africa before returning to India, where he was one of the leaders of the fight for his country's independence from the British. His policy of non-violent protest (including marches and hunger strikes) has been a model for political protest ever since.

Gandhi did not live to see independence in 1947. He was assassinated in 1946. *Gandhi: A Life* tells a story of great courage and integrity in a style that is easy to understand. Highly recommended.

Like Water in Wild Places is a book by Pamela Jooste about a brother and sister growing up in South Africa. Their brutal father is a member of the white government that practises apartheid (the subjugation of the black population). The brother is taught to hunt and ends up committing atrocities for the government before he realises how misguided he is. The sister rebels against the system and pays a terrible price. The book is the brother's journey to an understanding of what it all means.

Like Water in Wild Places is beautifully written. It tells its story without sentiment, but in a completely compelling way.

a What's the name of the book?		
b Who's the author?		
c Where and when does the story take place?		
d Who are the main characters?		
e What are the main events? / What is the plot of the book?		
f Would you recommend this book to someone else? Why or why not?		

2 Put the following words and phrases in order to make sentences about a novel called *Bel Canto* by the writer Ann Patchett

a a / a book / Ann Patchett, / about / *Bel Canto* /, / by / is / love in / siege. / terrorist

....

b a / a / birthday party / businessman. / for / It / Japanese / Mr Hosokawa, / starts off / with

....

c an / country. / house / in / is / It / Latin American / of / set in / the / the vice-president / unnamed

....

d music / a / tells / love / kidnapping. / story / terrorist / of / and / in the middle of / a / It

....

e fantastically / is / It / written.

....

f downable. / is / It / put- / un-

....

3 Read the following notes about *Bel Canto*. Use the information to write a quick report like the two in Activity 1.

What's the name of the book?	*Bel Canto*
Who's the author?	Ann Patchett
Where and when does the story take place?	• the house of the vice-president of an unnamed Latin American country • time: the present
Who are the main characters?	• Mr Hosokawa, a Japanese businessman who loves opera • Gen, his aide and translator • Rosanna Cox, an international opera star • the vice-president • a gang of kidnappers / terrorists • Carmen, a young terrorist
What are the main events? / What is the plot of the book?	• a party to celebrate Mr Hosokawa's birthday • Rosanna Cox has flown in to sing. • Terrorists take the guests hostage. • Two couples fall, improbably, in love. • at the end: death, hope
Would you recommend this book to someone else? Why or why not?	• Yes / No • fantastic writing • un-put-downable • music, love and fear: a perfect combination

....

....

....

....

....

...A When a crime is not a crime

1 Read about the 'crimes' and complete the table which follows.

Finders keepers?

Joey Coyle wasn't doing too well. He was a dockworker by trade, but he had been unemployed for some time. He had a drug problem too, and nothing went right for him. And even when it did, poor Joey managed to make a mess of it.

And then, on February 26th 1981, Joey, aged 28, spotted a yellow box on the side of a road in Philadelphia. He looked around but there was nobody who might be the owner of such a box. He thought about it for a moment and then decided to pick it up and take it home. He reckoned it would make a good toolbox.

Before taking the box home, he opened it. He expected it to be empty, but it wasn't. Instead, he found two bags inside with the words 'Reserve Bank' printed on them. With his pulse quickening, he pulled the bags open and found himself looking at over a million dollars in $100 bills. Joey stared and stared and then quickly put the bags into his car and drove away.

A few minutes later, an armoured money truck came roaring up to the place where the yellow box had been. The guards inside had realised that they had dropped the box out of the van and had come back to look for it. But of course it wasn't there, and they were left wondering how to explain to their company that they had mislaid a million dollars in cash.

Joey made a mess of his windfall as you might expect. One moment he was experiencing the euphoria of being rich beyond his wildest dreams, and next he was experiencing a bad case of paranoia about being discovered and having 'his' money taken away from him. He told everyone he met about his good luck and then swore them to secrecy. He had no idea what to do with the money, but his girlfriend put him in touch with gangster friends of hers who offered to help him invest it and make it grow. In his confusion, Joey trusted them and within only a short time the money had gone.

Joey had lost all the money he had found, but that didn't mean he wasn't guilty of committing a crime. In the state of Pennsylvania, you are committing an offence if you do not try to return things with a value of more than $250. The police finally caught up with him and Joey was arrested and thrown in jail, but he was released when a jury found him 'not guilty' because, they thought, he had become temporarily insane on finding the money. Sometime later, Joey's story was made into a Hollywood movie called *Money for Nothing*, starring John Cusack. Perhaps the unemployed dockworker's luck was about to change. But it was too late for Joey Coyle. He died before the film was released.

John Cusack as Joey Coyle in the film *Money for Nothing*.

Man 1 Bank 0

In 1995 Patrick Combs was living in San Francisco and trying desperately to make ends meet. He had just written a guide for college students called *Major in Success* and he was using the book to launch what he hoped would be a successful career as a motivational speaker, helping people to make the most of their talents and abilities. And no one needed his advice more than Patrick himself. Money had always been tight in Patrick's family and, at 28, he thought it was always going to be like that for him.

But you never know your luck! One day he found some junk mail that had been delivered to his mail box. He was going to throw it away, but instead he decided to give it a quick look before getting rid of it. He found himself looking at a letter promising that if he sent money to a certain company, he would soon be receiving huge cheques which would make him rich. And to prove it, the company had put a specimen cheque in with their letter – just to show their clients what riches would look like.

Patrick looked at the fake cheque despondently. It was a depressing reminder of how broke he was. But then he saw an opportunity for some fun. After all, he had nothing to lose. He thought it would be a funny joke to deposit the cheque in his account. He would give bank employees a laugh when they discovered that 'some idiot' had tried to cash a junk-mail cheque. So he giggled as he wrote in the amount of the deposit, $95,093.35, on the deposit slip. 'I didn't think I was sticking money into the bank,' he says. He didn't even bother to endorse the back by signing it as you are supposed to do.

After ten days, much to his shock, he found that the cheque had been cleared and the money had been credited to his account. (As he later learned, the cheque met the nine criteria of a valid cheque – and even the words 'non negotiable' printed on the front did not negate it.) The junk-mail company had succeeded in making the cheque look real – far too real. And to make matters worse for the bank, they had missed their own legal deadline to notify him that the cheque had bounced as a 'non-cash' item. With 'money' in his account, Patrick became obsessed. He couldn't think of anything else. 'It was an addiction,' he says, 'for two months I obsessed on whether I should take the money or give the money back.' After researching his own legal position long and hard, he discovered that he was not legally responsible for returning the money – he had committed no crime.

But in the end, Patrick decided to do the 'right' thing. He returned the money to the bank, but only after he had insisted (and the bank had agreed) that the bank would write him a letter confirming that they had made a mistake in cashing the cheque. Patrick had, by this time, become a celebrity and he used the story to catapult his career as a motivational speaker. Today his money worries are over.

To read the whole story visit www.man1bank0.com

	Finders keepers?	Man 1 Bank 0
a When and where did the story take place?		
b What was the name, age and occupation of the person in the story?		
c How much money did he get?		
d How did he get it?		
e Was he guilty of any crime?		
f What happened to the money?		
g What happened to the person in the story in the end?		

2 Match the *words* (*a–i*) with their meanings (*1–9*).

a euphoria   1 in short supply ....
b paranoia   2 accepted, recognised as valid ....
c stared   3 sign and make official ....
d roaring   4 looked keenly at something ....
e tight   5 extreme happiness ....
f giggled   6 the feeling that people are against you ....
g endorse   7 laughed happily ....
h cleared   8 promote very quickly ....
i catapult   9 driving fast and noisily ....

Language in chunks

3 Combine the words from the two circles to make phrases from the stories on pages 92 and 93. Three phrases start with *to make*.

a beyond his
b he had nothing
c his luck was
d nothing went
e to make
f to put someone
g to swear someone
h with his pulse

1 a mess of something
2 about to change
3 in touch with somebody
4 quickening
5 right for him
6 the most of something
7 to lose
8 to secrecy
9 wildest dreams
10 matters worse

4 Now use the phrases (or parts of the phrases) in the following sentences. You may have to change tenses, adjectives (e.g. *his*) or pronouns (e.g. *he* or *him*).

a .... Jennifer realised that she might have found the treasure she had been searching for since last week.

b After he had won the competition he found that he was rich ....

c After he left his job he found that .... anymore and so he decided to go back home.

d After years of poverty, and even though he didn't yet know it, George's ....

e He .... He said to her he would tell the world when he was ready, but until then he didn't want anyone else to know.

f One of the things I've enjoyed most is .... friends they haven't seen for years.

g People who .... of every opportunity are usually more successful than those who don't.

h She admitted that she had .... her exam paper. She was sure she'd failed.

i She burnt the toast and .... she spilt milk all over the kitchen floor.

j She thought she might as well try to escape from prison. After all she had ....

●● B   Coughing for a million

 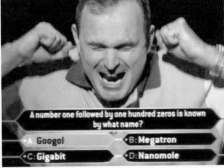 

Who wants to be a millionaire? has been one of the most popular television quiz shows, not only in Britain, but also around the world. In the show, the host asks a question and gives the contestant four possible answers. If the contestant gets the right answer, they win the money – say £100 – and then go on to the next question for, say, £250. The money increases for each question until, if the contestant has answered all the other questions correctly, the prize for the final question is one million pounds.

In this extract from a show some years ago, the host of the show is television personality Chris Tarrant. Answering the questions is an ex-army officer, Charles Ingram.

TARRANT: What kind of garment is an 'Anthony Eden'? An overcoat, hat, shoe, tie?
INGRAM: I think it is a hat.
A cough from the audience.
INGRAM: Again I'm not sure. I think it is ...
Coughing from the audience.
INGRAM: I am sure it is a hat. Am I sure?
Coughing from the audience.
INGRAM: Yes, hat, it's a hat.

That answer – the name for a peculiar type of British hat that nobody wears anymore – earned Charles Ingram £250,000. Two questions later, he had won a million pounds, and the audience in the studio went crazy. But something wasn't quite right. As he progressed through the various stages, Charles Ingram didn't really seem very sure of himself; he obviously didn't know the answer at first, so he must have been very good at guessing. Unless he wasn't guessing. To many in the audience that night, it seemed as if he kept changing his mind and frequently repeated an answer as if waiting for a signal.

He was.

Charles Ingram's wife Diana was in the audience, and so too was a man with the extraordinary name of Tecwen Whittock. At first, people might have been sympathetic about Tecwen. He had a bad cough. But a man sitting next to him in the audience noticed that there was something strange about the cough. It was too loud, and it wasn't very regular. It only happened occasionally, almost as if he was coughing on purpose.

He was.

The three of them, Charles Ingram, Diana Ingram and Tecwen Whittock, had planned the whole thing. Whittock coughed to tell Charles when he had the correct answer. They began to notice it in the television control room, but at first they didn't believe it. In the end, though, it was just too obvious, and when tapes from the programme were played to a court in London a year later, there was no doubt. Charles and Diana Ingram were guilty of cheating on a game show. They were given prison sentences of 18 months and fined £15,000 each. Tecwen Whittock was sentenced to 12 months in prison and fined £10,000. None of them actually went to prison, however, because the sentences were 'suspended' – that means that they would not go to prison unless they committed another crime.

Did the Ingrams and Tecwen Whittock get an appropriate sentence? How 'bad' is it to cheat a television quiz show in which winning money is a matter of chance anyway? It is crimes like this that challenge our notions of what is right and what is wrong, and since administering justice in the courts means that we have to decide on how serious something is (is robbery more or less serious than driving too fast, for example), the case of the cheating Ingrams is an excellent one to consider.

1   Read the extract from the book *Judging Crime* by Peter Hedley (page 95). Who or what is:

a ... *Who wants to be a millionaire?* ....

b ... Chris Tarrant? ....

c ... Charles Ingram? ....

d ... Tecwen Whittock? ....

2   Find the names of people or things.

a It was shown everywhere – not just in the UK. ....

b It is worth one million pounds. ....

c It is a kind of hat. ....

d It was worth £250,000. ....

e He didn't seem sure of himself. ....

f He coughed a lot of the time. ....

g They thought he was waiting for something. ....

h She was in the audience. ....

i He noticed that there was something strange about the cough. ....

j They had planned the whole thing. ....

k They were shown to people during the trial. ....

l They were fined a total of £30,000. ....

m He was given a 12 months' suspended sentence. ....

3   Complete each blank with one word from the text. Do not change the word in any way.

a A .... is someone who invites you to their house, or to a party, or who is in charge of an event like a quiz show.

b A .... is someone who takes part in a race or a game.

c If something gets bigger or more dangerous, for example, we say that it ....

d An .... is part of a whole.

e .... is a formal word for an article of clothing.

f If something happens every few minutes, with the same interval of time between each occurrence, we say that it is ....

g When someone does something because they want to do it, we can say they have done it

....

h When something is very clear so that anyone can understand it, we say that it is ....

i The word .... can either mean the place where a trial takes place or the people who are in the place where a trial takes place.

j If something is correct and suitable for a situation or an event, we say that it is ....

k Tina was in charge of .... the charity's budget of a million pounds.

l Those two students were copying each other's work in the exam. They were ....

●●C Editing

1 **Read what these students of English say about writing. Tick the boxes to show if you agree or disagree with what they say.**

	Agree	Disagree
I always check what I have written to look for mistakes.		
The content of what I write is just as important as not making mistakes.		
I use my dictionary to check spelling.		
I try to show what I write in English to someone else, before I send it or hand it in to a teacher.		
I don't worry about my spelling in emails.		

2 **Look at the advertisement and read the letter that a student wrote in answer to it. Complete the form on page 98 about the letter.**

THE CRIME PAGE

Do you know of any famous or unusual crimes? We'd love to hear about them. Send the facts to famouscrimes@thisweek.com
If we publish your story, we'll send you a year's free subscription to our magazine.

Dear Editor,

I want tell you about a famous crime. This crime happen in my home town of Guadalajara five years ago. A little boy was kidnap. People was sure it was the family driver who did take the boy and the father get mad and fired the driver. But the mother of the boy knew he couldn't had done it. She trusted the driver. Then, sudenly, the father disappeared. Nobody knew where he did go. The police looked for man and they found him at the airport. He was trying leave the country with the boy. The police gave the boy back to his mother and the father went to the jail.

Juan Manuel Alvarez

3 Complete the form about Juan Manuel's letter.

Name of writer:			
	Yes	More or less	No, not really
a Is the writing interesting?			
b Does the writing contain enough information?			

c Juan Manuel could improve this letter if

1 ....

2 ....

4 Correct the mistakes highlighted in yellow in the letter.

a ....

b ....

c ....

d ....

e ....

f ....

g ....

h ....

i ....

j ....

k ....

l ....

5 Write your own letter about a famous crime, in draft form, and then complete the following tasks.

a Read the letter as if it was someone else's. Copy and complete the table in Activity 3 about your own writing.

b Look for any mistakes and correct them.

c Write a final 'clean' copy of your letter.

A Stories in poems

1 Cover the poems below. Look at these three titles.
  Complete the boxes with words you would expect to see.

Midsummer, Tobago

Like a Beacon

Handbag

Derek Walcott

Grace Nichols

Ruth Fainlight

Read the poems. Did you guess any of the words?

Midsummer, Tobago

Broad sun-stoned beaches.

White heat.
A green river.

A bridge, scorched yellow palms

from the summer-sleeping house
drowsing through August.

Days I have held,
days I have lost,

days that outgrow, like daughters,
my harbouring arms.

Derek Walcott

Like a Beacon
In London
every now and then
I get this craving
for my mother's food
I leave art galleries
in search of plantains
saltfish / sweet potatoes

I need this touch of home
swinging my bag
like a beacon
against the cold

Grace Nichols

Handbag
My mother's old leather handbag,
crowded with letters she carried
all through the war. The smell
of my mother's handbag: mints
and lipstick and Coty powder.
The look of those letters, softened
and worn at the edges, opened,
read, and refolded so often.
Letters from my father. Odour
of leather and powder, which ever
since then has meant womanliness,
and love, and anguish, and war.

Ruth Fainlight

2 Explain the meaning of the following words and expressions.

Midsummer, Tobago

a broad ....

b scorched ....

c summer-sleeping house ....

d drowsing ....

e outgrow ....

f harbouring ....

Like a Beacon

g craving ....

h plantains ....

i touch of home ....

j swinging ....

k beacon ....

Handbag

l crowded with letters ....

m lipstick ....

n powder ....

o softened and worn at the edges ....

p odour ....

q womanliness ....

r anguish ....

3 In your own words, write three things that are the same about the
poems and three differences between them.

Similarities

a ....

b ....

c ....

Differences

a ....

b ....

c ....

B *Why Cat and Dog are no longer friends*

1 Read the introduction. Where did West Indian folk tales come from originally, and how were they changed?

....

....

....

When the Europeans brought West Africans to the West Indies to work for them, the Africans brought their stories with them, stories from the Ashanti people about Anansi the spider and all the other animals. But in the West Indies, these stories changed and new animals were added: Snake, Rat, Cat, Dog, Parrot, Tumble-bug and Turtle. These stories – or folk tales – are still told today.

One of the most popular stories is called *Why Cat and Dog are no longer friends*.

2 Read the paragraphs on this and the next page. Put them in the right order. The first two are done for you.

[ ] 'Dog,' said one of the other cats, 'this isn't like you. Why are you shouting at us like this? It isn't dignified, and it's not a bit like you, and besides, I think you'd better get back to the house. It seems to be on fire.'

[ ] 'Good idea,' said Dog. 'Let's talk about it when I've finished making the dinner.' He left the room and went to the fire to complete the cooking. Meanwhile, Finger Quashy went to the pantry where she saw, to her delight, that there were two beautiful pears on a top shelf. She took them down, leapt out of the window, and hid them in the garden so she could take them home later. But unfortunately for her, Rat saw her take the pears and started yelling his head off. 'Dog,' he shouted, 'oh, Dog. Finger Quashy has taken your pears. Finger Quashy has stolen your pears.'

[ ] And that's why Dog and Cat are no longer friends. Dog blamed the four Cats for distracting him so that the house burnt down, and he suspected, anyway, that Rat had been right about Finger Quashy. Worst of all, all his clothes had been reduced to ashes in the fire and he only had one suit left – the one he was wearing (which was the one he was born in) – and which he would have to wear until he died.

[ ] But Dog wasn't having any of it. He was absolutely beside himself with fury and he had a great big stick in his hand. He was ready to kill somebody.

[ ] Dog looked back, and it was true. Flames were ripping through the kitchen and he could hear his young son calling for help. He ran back into the house, saved his son and ran back into the garden. The Cats had gone. Dog had to watch his house, with all his things, burn right down to the ground. It turned out that his son had been playing with the fire, and because he wasn't there he hadn't realised until it was too late.

[ ] Finger Quashy was right to be nervous. Dog was at his wits' end. Every time he put pears out to ripen in the sun, someone stole them. He swore that if he ever found out who the thief was, he would break their bones. So when the Cats arrived, dressed in their finest clothes, Finger Quashy said, 'Dog, it's a real problem about your pears. I reckon it's Rat who's taking them, and since I'm the fastest cat around, why don't you make me your watchwoman and then I can guard your pears and stop Rat getting them?'

[ ] One of the things that Finger Quashy liked stealing most were the avocado pears that grew in Dog's garden. They were the most delicious pears for miles – and pears were the favourite food of all the cats in the area.

[ ] The Cats didn't need to think about it. They shot straight out of the window and into the garden where they scrambled up into a tree. Dog ran out after them and stood at the bottom of the tree, swearing in the most reprehensible fashion.

[2] The reason that Finger Quashy was nervous was that she feared that Dog might just know her secret. This was – and there is no nicer or kinder way to say it – that Finger Quashy was a thief. She stole everything all the time, but nobody knew about this because she was the fastest cat in those parts, and ran like the wind.

[ ] This was looking pretty bad for Finger Quashy, but she was, as we know, pretty fast. So she ran back into the sitting room, and by the time Dog came in, she was sitting there looking sweet, just like her three companions.

[1] When Dog invited four Cats to dinner, they were very pleased. He made good dinners and they were looking forward to a very nice meal. But one of the Cats was just a little bit nervous. Her name was Finger Quashy.

---

3 **Answer the following questions. Why:**

a ... was Finger Quashy nervous?

b ... did Dog's house burn down?

c ... did all the cats scramble up into the tree?

d ... was Dog so upset even before the dinner started?

e ... did Finger Quashy run back and sit in her chair looking nice?

f ... did Dog think that Finger Quashy had taken his pears?

g ... were the cats pleased to be asked for dinner?

h ... aren't Cat and Dog friends anymore?

i ... was Finger Quashy such a good thief?

j ... did Finger Quashy steal pears from Dog's garden (rather than other gardens)?

4 **Match the following definitions to words and expressions from the text in blue.**

   a a phrase that means that something is burning strongly

   ....

   b a phrase which means that a thing burned so fiercely that now it is just dust

   ....

   c a slightly old-fashioned word to describe the room where you keep food supplies

   ....

   d a word that means 'behaving in a calm, serious and appropriate way'

   ....

   e a word that means 'jumped in order to land in a different place'

   ....

   f a word to describe behaviour which is very bad and which people will criticise

   ....

   g a word which means 'taking somebody's attention away from something'

   ....

   h a word which means 'shouting and using bad words to insult people'

   ....

   i a word which means that you considered someone to be responsible for something bad

   ....

   j a word which means 'travelled at a fantastic speed'

   ....

   k an expression that means that it is not the way you usually behave

   ....

   l an expression which means that someone just has no idea what to do because nothing works

   ....

   m an expression which means 'shouting loudly in an uncontrolled way'

   ....

   n an expression which means 'very very angry indeed'

   ....

•••C Films

1 Read the film script and put the storyboards (the director's sketches for how the film will look) in the right order. Write numbers *1–6*.

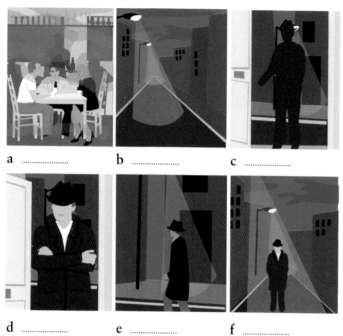

a .... b .... c ....

d .... e .... f ....

SCENE 1

Exterior. Night. Ten years ago. A small side street in a city. Pools of light from street lights. We see a figure walk through one of light pools towards us. He has a hat pulled down over his eyes. The camera follows the figure as he walks past us.

SCENE 2

Interior. The same night. A smoky café. Crowded. People sit at tables, talking furtively. They're all waiting for something perhaps. Edgy. The camera pans over the tables until it gets to the door. Which opens. Silhouetted in the street lamp from outside stands the figure we saw in Scene 1.

2 Read the film scenes again. Find:

a ... nine examples of sentences without verbs.

....

b ... a word that means 'the opposite of interior'.

....

c ... a phrase that means 'illuminated circles on the pavement'.

....

d ... a word that means 'a human' when we can't make out their physical appearance very well.

....

e ... a word that means there are a lot of people in a small space.

....

f ... a word that means 'secretly'.

....

g ... a word that means 'tense, nervous'.

....

h ... a verb used to say that a camera moves across a scene from one side to the other.

....

i ... a word that means 'with light behind' someone or something, so that we can't make out any details.

....

3   Look at the following storyboards and write two film scenes in the
    same way as those in Activity 1. Try and use as many of the words
    and phrases in the box as you can, and also words from the
    previous film scenes.

aerial shot
bright sunlight
glittering surf
heavy breathing
palm trees
to pitch forward
to trip
white sand

SCENE 1

SCENE 2

SCENE 1

SCENE 2

ANSWER KEY

UNIT 1

A 1
a 3
b 5
c 2
d 7
e 6
f 1
g 4

A 2

Brett
a busboy
b sales clerk
c $2 million
d He lent or spent all his money.
e huge credit card debts

Lynette
f bookkeeper
g $17 million
h She and her husband fought over money.
i She divorced her husband.

John and Sandy
j accountants
k $12 million
l Their kids lost their friends.
m They worried about safety.
n They lost their jobs.

A 3
a didn't like, was opposed to
b sudden unexpected piece of luck
c makes one feel isolated or not part of a community
d in an intelligent way
e terrible, very bad
f use up, wipe out
g from one day to the next, very suddenly

A 4
a time on her hands
b to make matters worse
c Money is no object.
d ended up
e way too much
f a dream come true

B 1
a someone who doesn't like to spend money at all
b someone who spends money easily
c doing something well
d someone who takes a lot of chances and risks

B 3
a penny-pincher
b on the right track
c daredevil
d spendthrift

B 4
a raffle
b tempted by
c can't be bothered to
d statements
e amid the clutter
f wardrobe
g keep track of
h extravagant
i manageable

B 5
a statement
b can't be bothered to
c wardrobe
d extravagant
e amid the clutter
f raffle
g manageable
h keep track of
i tempted by

C 1
The answer is a.

UNIT 2

A 1
The correct answer is a.

A 2
a This sentence does not fit in the text.
b 1
c 6
d 5
e 4
f 2
g 3

A 3
a white student at Little Rock's Central High School
b – shouted at a black student
 – apologised
 – reconciled
c – 1957
 – 1962
 – 1997
d photographer
e – took photo of black student entering white school
 – took photo of Hazel and Elizabeth
f – 1957/1997
g president, USA
h awarded medal to black students
i 1997
j president, USA
k – took control of National Guard
 – sent federal troops out
l 1957
m governor, Arkansas
n sent soldiers to stop black students
o 1957
p black student at Little Rock
q – first of nine black students at Little Rock school
 – met Hazel
r – 1957
 – 1997

A 4
a 3
b 4
c 7
d 1
e 6
f 5
g 2

A 5
a She never lost her composure when the police arrested her.
b It's a fact of life that everybody gets colds and flu from time to time.
c The Industrial Revolution changed the course of history.

d I can never fully repay my debt to you.
e I am bitterly opposed to your plan.
f They built new flood defences in the wake of the terrible storm. / In the wake of the terrible storm, they built new flood defences.
g When he saw the people in the stadium, he knew there would be trouble.

B 1
a Maurice Gatsonides
b Walter Arnold
c 30 miles an hour
d 80%

B 2
a 9
b 2
c 1
d 7
e 4
f 8
g 12
h 5
i 3
j 11
k 10
l 6

B 3
a activated
b Sensors
c surface
d device
e phenomenon
f built-up
g toll
h uncontroversial
i joyriders
j black spot

C 1
a
Possible answers
– There's going to be a big change in charges for parking cars.
– A family was caught in a fire and escaped because a smoke detector warned them about the fire.
– A photographer who took a famous photo at Little Rock has died.
– Someone suspected of killing someone in a photo booth has been arrested.
– A horse belonging to the Queen won a race, but it was a very close race.

b
Articles are often left out. The present tense is common.

C 2
Possible answers
– River plunge mother escapes injury
– Mother of three escapes injury in car river plunge
– Mother rescued by passing cyclist
– Cyclist dives in river, pulls woman from car
– Mystery hero saves mother in river plunge

C 3
– student, photographs, shock, robbers, bank, police
– singer, airport, attack, photographer, sue

C 4
Possible answers
– Student's photo in robbery shock
– Lucky shot for police
– Bank robbers caught by student's photo
– Singer attacks photographer in airport row
– Photographer threats to sue after airport attack

UNIT 3

A 1
The correct answer is b.

A 2
a because they killed their livestock
b a character in a fairy story
c a musical fable (by Prokofiev)
d the devil
e bones and twigs
f lions
g Romulus

A 3
a keep out of my way
b in the end
c do my best
d get my hands on
e just for the fun of it
f for a start
g ashamed of yourself

B 1
a 13 stallion
b 3 cow
c 5 dog
d 7 goat
e 9 koala bear
f 11 sheep
g 12 snake
h 8 kangaroo
i 1 alien
j 2 bat
k 10 ostrich
l 6 galah
m 14 wolf
n 15 wombat
o 4 crocodile

B 2
a stallion
b cows
c dogs
d goat
f sheep
g snake
h kangaroos
i aliens
l galah
n wombats

B 3
a Yes. She stared and stared. Kathryn says it was worth going 13,000 miles to surprise her.
b Yes. He tried to be cool but he was 'lost for words'.
c No. She describes him as a 'runaway husband' and later talks about her divorce.
d Yes. He had grown a lot since he used to be the same height as Kathryn.
e No. There were a lot of stars.
f No. It just says they were armed with a camera.
g No. She makes a joke about taking pictures of aliens, but it was probably just a photograph of cows.
h Yes. She says her stay at home wasn't long enough.
i No. She flew via Bali and Kuala Lumpur (and caught different planes).

B 4
a 8, 14
b 5
c 3
d 16
e 10
f 12
g 11
h 17, 1
i 2
j 15
k 13
l 6, 4
m 7
n 9

C 1
a The student isn't really in favour of zoos. He or she thinks proper wildlife parks are better.
b but – however
and – and furthermore
and – moreover
but – on the other hand
and – not only that, but
so – therefore
but – in contrast
so – as a result
so – in conclusion
but – nevertheless

C 3
Example plan
1 Introduction: introduce topic – discuss zoos, need for protection of species, rapid rate of extinction of species. How can animals best be protected?
Language: *I'd like to start by outlining the problem.*
2 For: arguments for zoos as best protection
Language: *Many people believe … It is true that …*
3 Against: arguments for other forms of protection / conservation
Language: *On the other hand … However …*
4 Conclusion: decide for one argument or the other
Language: *In conclusion therefore … Finally … To sum up …*

UNIT 4

A 1
Text 1
a Dustin Webster
b America
c cliff diving
d dive from very high; very dangerous
e saw high-divers aged 11
f member of high-diving team
g lost the latest contest
Text 2
a Audrey Mestre
b 11/8/74, France
c freediving
d dive very deep without oxygen
e mother / grandfather spearfishers
f set world record in May 2000
g died trying to set new record

A 2
a verb – launch = throw
b noun – piece = bit, small part
c adjective – frail = weak
d adjective – vulnerable = able to be hurt / unprotected
e noun – thesis = a piece of research turned into a written report
f noun – scuba-diving = underwater swimming with air tanks
g noun – apparatus = equipment

B 1
a 4
b 7
c 5
d 6
e 2
f 1
g 3

B 2
a F
b F
c T
d F
e T
f F
g F
h T
i T
j F

B 3
a daredevil
b thermos flask
c synonymous with
d ultimate
e obsessed with
f freight
g stigma
h transatlantic

C 1   **C 2**
a 8   a 3
b 9   b 9
c 10   c 2
d 5   d 7
e 7   e 5
f 4   f 8
g 3   g 4
h 2   h 10
i 1   i 6
j 6   j 1

UNIT 5

A 1
a secondary to some other emotion
b a way of displacing fear
c if the limbic parts of their brains are stimulated
d inheritance plays a part, as does our upbringing
e anger leads to an increased risk of heart attack
f suppressing anger is bad
g using anger consciously is a good thing

A 2
a F
b T
c T
d F
e T
f F

A 3
a Learn how to be assertive rather than aggressive
b Empathise with the other person
c Surround yourself with positive people
d Monitor your thoughts for traces of cynicism and general discontent
e Use your imagination, not your voice
f Change what you expect
g Stop the clock

A 4
a use your imagination
b play a part
c bad for people
d out of control
e as a way of
f take a deep breath
g on the surface

B 1
a Petra Weiss
b Hugh Foster
c Bud Karlowski
d Felicity Poole
e Miriam Stirling
f Sarah Green
g Bob Cartwright

h   Carl Preston
i   Katie Davis
j   Phil Discarson
k   Danuta Ross
l   Caroline Hartley

B 2
a   a newspaper's website
b/c Carl Preston, Sarah Greene and Felicity Poole are a little more serious than the others, as they quote scientific research. The other answers are not meant to be taken seriously.
d   The following opinions are in *Notes & Queries*: 2, 3 and 5

B 3
a   in better condition
b   depends on
c   as far back as
d   pretending
e   appropriate facial expressions
f   get the message
g   physical manifestations
h   laughter lines
i   villain
j   free time
k   burn calories
l   tell jokes

C 1
Possible answers
–   Name of the place described: Aroma
–   What kind of a place it is: It's a centre where people can do different relaxing things.
–   Services offered: courses in aromatherapy (using smells to make people feel good), Feng Shui (learning where to put things in a house), relaxing colour (using colour to relax people)
–   Names of the staff: Sally Grace, Justin Knocker, Helena Kollect
–   Address, phone number, website, etc.: 20 Carper Row, Middleton, Cleethorpe, Lancs LT6 5YW, 01672 462057, www.arofengcol.com
–   How many sheets make up the leaflet: three sheets are visible

C 2
a   Sebastian West
b   Kylie Strachan
c   Christopher Major
d   David Jones
e   175 Harbour Walk
f   Lowminster LH3 5YT
g   017583 444456
h   info@muswork.org.uk
i   www.muswork.org.uk
j   music appreciation classes
k   instrumental classes on a range of instruments
l   3 orchestras
m   Saturday concerts

UNIT 6

A 1
a   7
b   4
c   6
d   1
e   3
f   5
g   8
h   2

A 2
a   because he said that we had reached the limits of what we could do with technology (wrong), but also that his

statement would sound silly in five years' time (right)
b   mapping the human genome; extraction of stem cells
c   The doctor operated by remote control.
d   because it's too cold and dry
e   by warming it up and planting trees to make oxygen
f   within the next 80 years

A 3
a   5
b   4
c   1
d   7
e   6
f   3
g   2

A 4
a   a long way off
b   warm up
c   by that time
d   dismiss … as
e   scoot around
f   tend to
g   spewing out

A 5
Possible answers
a   We will fly using our own wings.
b   Men will have babies.
c   The Earth will become extinct.
d   We will be living on Mars in the next 80 years.
e   We will have planted trees on Mars.

B 1		B 2	
a	5	a	6
b	6	b	2
c	3	c	4
d	4	d	5
e	2	e	1
f	1	f	3

B 3
a   a conference and exhibition of technology
b   a pop artist
c   a Chinese artist
d   someone who reads cards to tell your fortune
e   a session when someone (who claims to have special talents) tells you what they 'see' is going to happen in your future
f   someone who takes advantage of the generosity of others by accepting material things and offering nothing in return
g   a famous astrologer and predictor of the future
h   the end of the world
i   the temperature on Saturday in London

B 4
a   information technology
b   electronic entertainment, electronic marketing – connected with entertainment and marketing online
c   Tuesday–Sunday
d   non-traditional, experimental
e   someone who can see into the future
f   predictions
g   spending time with you
h   west south west (direction of the wind)
i   miles per hour
j   73 degrees Fahrenheit – a measure of temperature used in the USA

C 1
Possible answer
In the year 2050, I'll be living on Mars. Even though I'll be 70 years old, I'll still be young, because scientists will have found a

way for us to live forever. I'll get up when my robot comes to wake me and bring me coffee in bed and my breakfast. My breakfast will be just some pills. All food on Mars will be dehydrated, because nothing will grow there. I'll think up (dial) my friends on Earth and on the Moon on my TPP (telepathy phone) and we'll talk while I get ready for work.

UNIT 7

A 1		A 2	
a	5	a	2
b	3	b	2
c	1	c	3
d	2	d	1
e	4	e	2

A 3
a   derive
b   elicits
c   complement
d   nurturing
e   conventional
f   chilling out
g   vibrations
h   contract
i   adamant
j   inadvertently

A 4
a   affects us
b   look for different ways of
c   causes a strong reaction
d   polite, well-behaved
e   is entitled to

A 5
a   Brilliant sunshine has a bad effect on me.
b   Interior designers are seeking new ways of combining colours.
c   The colour red elicits a strong psychological response in bulls.
d   When their grandmother comes to tea, the children are always on their best behaviour.
e   No one has the right to order me about.

B 2
a   Each hat represents a different way of looking at a problem.
b   to focus on the problem, not the individual, to look at a problem in many different ways, to allow a group of people to think effectively about a problem at the same time

B 4
–   white: facts and true information
–   red: intuition, feelings and emotions – how you feel about something
–   black: logic, judgment, caution, analysis – what can work and why, what won't work and why not
–   yellow: positive reason, suggestions and proposals – advantages of the suggestions
–   green: creativity, alternatives, combinations of ideas – more ideas are generated
–   blue: metacognition, thinking about thinking – tells the group what kind of thinking still needs to take place

B 5
a   7
b   3
c   1
d   2
e   6
f   4

g 8
h 2
C 1
a using facts and evidence
b follow a series of logical steps
c a 'right' answer
d an original, creative solution
e think in different directions and come up with answers that don't have to be logical
f not necessarily one correct answer
C 2
a 1 Some people think colours have an effect on our mood; however, not everyone believes this to be true.
   2 Some people think colours have an effect on our mood. Nevertheless, not everyone believes this to be true.
b 1 The best colour for a person with blue eyes to wear is blue, while the best colour for someone with green eyes to wear is green.
   2 The best colour for a person with blue eyes to wear is blue, whereas the best colour for someone with green eyes to wear is green.
   3 The best colour for a person with blue eyes to wear is blue, compared to green which is the best colour for someone with green eyes to wear.
c 1 Both people with green eyes and people with hazel eyes can wear shades of green.
   2 People with green eyes can wear shades of green and people with hazel eyes can too.
d 1 A Luscher test can be taken online. Likewise, it can be taken in person.
   2 A Luscher test can be taken online. Similarly, it can be taken in person.
C 3
Possible answers

Both logical and lateral thinking can be very effective. However, lateral thinking asks you to 'think outside the box' and look for original, creative solutions to problems. The idea is to think in different directions, and to come up with answers that are not necessarily logical. While logical thinking assumes one correct answer, lateral thinking assumes that the logical answer is not always the appropriate answer or that there is not just one 'right' answer.

C 4
Possible answer

Both left-brain and right-brain dominance have advantages and disadvantages. When solving problems, left-brain dominant people tend to be intellectual and use logic, while right-brain dominant people are more likely to be intuitive and use their feelings. Right-brain dominant people remember faces, whereas left-brain dominant people remember names. In thinking, people who are left-brain dominant usually use language, compared to the images that right-brain dominant people use to help them to think. Finally, left-brain dominant people are more likely to control their feelings. Right-brain dominant people, on the other hand, are usually more free with their feelings.

UNIT 8
A 1
a 3
b 4
c 2
d 1
A 2
a Dr Mercola
b vegans
c Greenpeace
d Monsanto
e vegans / Dr Mercola (he says 'for certain health conditions')
f Monsanto
g Greenpeace
A 3
a 4
b 5
c 8
d 6
e 9
f 3
g 1
h 7
i 11
j 2
k 10
A 4
a condition, illness, sickness, disease, hunger
b terrorism, hunger, disease, fat, animal products, poverty, living longer, dying earlier
c wave of rejection, hunger, terrorism, poverty
d hunger, illness, poverty
e destroying, winning, producing, living longer
f emotion, protein, fat, animal products, vitamins
g sickness, disease, terrorism, poverty, dying earlier, living longer
A 5
a global poverty
b devoid of animal products / fat
c linked to living longer
d a debilitating illness / condition / sickness / disease
e intent on winning
f stave off hunger
g associated with dying earlier
B 1
Dr Arthur Agatson: The South Beach Diet
Dr Robert Atkins: The Atkins Diet
Bernice Weston: Weight Watchers of Great Britain
Dr Barry Sears: The Zone Diet
B 2
a carbohydrates found in processed foods
b Bernice Weston
c Arthur Agatson
d Barry Sears
e people on the induction phase of the Atkins Diet
f fruits and vegetables which contain a lot of fibre
g members of Weight Watchers
h Robert Atkins
i monounsaturated fats found in olive and canola oils, meat and seafood
j *People* magazine
k Weight Watchers
l Robert Atkins

B 3
a 2
b 3
c 4
d 1
B 4
a 3
b 8
c 5
d 7
e 2
f 6
g 1
h 4
B 5
a 3
b 4
c 1
d 2
B 6
a 5
b 6
c 4
d 1
e 8
f 7
g 3
h 2
C 1
a part 3
b part 1
c part 2
C 2
Possible answer
Part 1

This table shows the results of a survey carried out by Australian High School students, in which 200 people were asked whether, in their opinion, the dangers of genetic modification of plants were more important than the possible advantages.
Part 2

The results show that 24% of the people asked felt that the dangers were more important than the advantages, while nearly half (44%) thought the dangers were not as important as the advantages. However, about a third (32%) said they didn't know the answer to the question.
Part 3

This seems to show that a majority of people in Australia either are not worried by the genetic modification of plants, or simply don't have an opinion.

UNIT 9
A 1
Advantages
better social life, as they are considered more attractive and more feminine
Disadvantages
worse career prospects (more likely to be rejected, lower salary), as they are considered less intelligent, less mature and less capable, because blondness gives a child-like appearance
A 2
a almost half of women
b peroxide
c people who are asked to rate others for 'attractiveness'
d Diana Kayle
e brunettes
f blond hair, according to one theory
g Brian Bates' business students
h Brian Bates' business stduents
i men
A 3
a applicant
b CV
c equally qualified
d reject
e appointed
f salary
g PA
A 4
a Most blondes use bottles of hair dye to make their hair blonde.
b While being blonde may boost your social life, it can also be bad for your possible future career.
c It's almost impossible to believe that such changeable features as hair colour

could so influence recruitment decisions.

d The picture, for me, wasn't one of the deciding factors.

e I did my best to ignore the appearance of the applicants.

f When they were asked detailed questions, they revealed that the … stereotype had … affected their judgement.

B 1
a Nick Drake
b 1948–1974
c 3
d 1 Brad Pitt, 2 Coldplay,
  3 Beth Orton, 4 Norah Jones

B 2
a Tonya Swift
b Jesse
c Sarah Beatrice
d Usha Jain
e Lucy Sparrow
f Bentley
g Alejandra's friend
h Alejandra Valero
i Lucy Sparrow

B 3
a *Man in a shed*
b *Time of no reply*
c *Pink moon*
d *Way to blue*
e *Cello song*

B 4
a background
b captivated
c entangled
d timeless
e melancholic
f haunting
g inspirational
h uplifting
i missions

C 1
a F (It was October – the 10th month.)
b T
c F (He is still waiting for the results.)
d F (He did worse in Music and Physics.)
e F (He has 10.)
f F (He works at a clothing store; a department store sells everything.)
g F
h T
i F (It says 'part-time'.)
j F (He plays the guitar.)
k F (He goes to 'home' games.)
l T

C 2
a 1975
b Camelthorpe Primary School
c Parkridge Community College
d Leeds University
e Camelthorpe College of Further Education
f History
g Art
h English Literature
i Diploma in journalism
j History (2:1)
k 2001 – Reporter, *Daily Mirror*
l 1997–2001 Reporter, *Camelthorpe Daily News*
m 2001 (July & August) McDonald's (full-time)
n 1994–1998 Post Office (Christmas holiday period)
o 1993–1994 Gap year (Tanzania)
p I'm keen on football. I support Chelsea.

I play tennis and I paint for fun (as an amateur).

q I think my experience equips me perfectly for the job. The work I have done for the *Daily Mirror* (see attached documents) corresponds exactly to what is expected in this job. Colleagues will tell you I get on well with people. I enjoy the atmosphere of a busy working newspaper.

r Morgan Peters
s *Camelthorpe Daily News*

UNIT 10

A 1
a 12
b 9
c 6
d 5
e 4
f 8
g 10
h 3
i 2
j 7
k 11
l 1

A 2
It appears that Eleanor enjoyed the evening. She uses expressions like *exciting, terrific dinner, really beautiful*. She describes the children playing happily, etc.

A 3
a thunder
b roast
c intersection
d staged
e flooded
f streaming
g soaked
h waded
i fabulous

A 4
a Because they liked the way it moved under their feet.
b Because they couldn't get home.
c Because the water was six inches deep in the room.
d Because he'd had to walk through the rain.
e Because there wasn't enough meat for everyone.
f Because dirt from the garden was flowing into it.
g Because the thunder and the rain were so loud.
h Because there was no electricity.
i Because they can compensate for low levels of light.
j Because when the electricity came back, all the appliances in the house came on.

A 5
a the carpet looked like it was floating; the kids thought it looked like a water bed
b to make it home
c turned on *La Bohème* full volume
d now and then
e they had bananas flambé by candlelight
f eyes can compensate for the low level of light

B 2
Possible answer
The effects of global warming are slowly becoming apparent. If we do not deal with the problem now, by the time the effects of

global warming manifest themselves clearly, it will be too late.

B 3		B 4	
a	RL	a	1
b	M	b	2
c	RL	c	2
d	SP	d	3
e	RL	e	1
f	SP	f	3
g	RL	g	1
h	SP	h	2
i	M	i	1
j	RL		

C 1
The correct answer is b.

C 2
April 15th
a Mole's boss
b Mole
c His bicycle was stolen.
d sarcastic
May 24th
a Because of a dog who might be dangerous.
b on the surface, friendly
c that the dog will bite his face
d related to what he thinks might happen if the dog bites him
May 25th
a Oxford
b ride on the tops of buses, walk along looking upwards and ask the way
c sending them the wrong way
d …

UNIT 11

A 1
a Shows that go into someone's home. – *The Osbournes*
b Shows that put people into an unusual situation. – *Joe Millionaire, The Real World*
c Shows where people talk about their personal problems. – *Jerry Springer, Judge Judy*
d Shows where people go on dates with strangers. – *Eliminate, Blind Date*

A 2
a F
b T
c F
d T
e T
f F
g F
h T
i T

A 3
a making money from something
b the number of people who watch TV shows
c feature / have in the central role
d keen
e invented and made
f likely to cause arguments
g dangerous, embarrassing
h occasions when they are seen by the public

A 4
a to reveal all
b jumped at the chance
c no qualms about
d no limits about
e were reassured
f With the growth of
g one by one

A 5
a   4
b   1
c   2
d   3
e   look at, get along with, take off
f   take off
g   get along with
h   give away

A 6
a   taken off
b   get along with
c   look at
d   give away

B 1
Friends: b, h, k
Art of the garden: f, i
Big Brother – Live Launch Show: a, d, e, j
American Idol: c, g, l

B 2
a   Alison Graham
b   Capability Brown
c   the *Big Brother* programme makers
d   Fantasia Barrino and Diana DeGarmo
e   *American Idol*
f   the character 'Joey' from *Friends*
g   *Big Brother*
h   Phoebe in *Friends*
i   the last episode of *Friends*
j   Diarmuid Gavin
k   the Duke of Blenheim
l   Diarmuid Gavin
m   Cameron Stuart
n   Cameron Stuart

B 3
a   bid their last farewells
b   tying-up of loose ends
c   there are no great fireworks
d   talks us through
e   dark horse
f   fell out with
g   pulls in big audiences
h   brickbats
i   fool the eye
j   we'll just have to wait and see
k   crowning achievement
l   as dull as ditchwater

C 2

	A	B
a	1954	2
b	stuntman	8
c	famous all over the world	11
d	how to perform stunts	7
e	He hated it.	5
f	biggest Hong Kong film star in Hollywood	10
g	adding comedy	9
h	China Drama Academy	6
i	Hong Kong	1
j	Hong Kong	4
k	cook and housekeeper	3

C 3
Possible answer
Shakira was born in Barranquilla, Colombia on 2 February, 1977. Her real name is Shakira Mebarak Ripoll. Her mother is Colombian and her father is Lebanese.

She started writing songs at the age of eight and signed her first recording contract in 1990 at the age of 13. She is famous for developing her own style of music, which combines her Latin and Arabic influences with modern rock music.

Today she is famous worldwide with best-selling records in English, Spanish and even in Portuguese.

UNIT 12
A 1
a   4
b   1
c   2
d   3

A 2
a   Will's father
b   Marcus's Mum (and Marcus)
c   Will
d   Marcus
e   Marcus's Mum
f   Nick Hornby
g   Will
h   Marcus

A 3
a   the large area of land near an island
b   unfashionable
c   very happily
d   huge
e   sports shoes
f   said of what someone used to do or be
g   gives us
h   certain
i   trying hard

A 4
a   3
b   2
c   7
d   5
e   4
f   1
g   6

A 5
a   settled down
b   to face up to
c   from a mile off
d   figure of fun
e   awe-inspiring
f   relate to
g   didn't mind admitting it

A 6
Paula
a   Isabel Allende
b   autobiography
c   While Isabel Allende's daughter, Paula, is in a coma, Allende tells the story of her family.
d   Beautiful, moving, fascinating, rich prose.

The Green Mile
e   Stephen King
f   novel (thriller)
g   There is a new prisoner at Cold Mountain prison and the book tells the story of this man.
h   Makes the reader want to read more, haunting.

B 1
The correct summary is c.

B 2
a   1
b   1
c   3
d   1
e   2
f   2
g   1

B 3
a   fork
b   tights
c   scratch
d   to squat
e   I'd got that far.
f   to groan
g   blockage

h   to poke out
i   to stack up
j   to slice
k   to tune
l   leaf

C 1
a   – *Gandhi: A Life*
    – *Like Water in Wild Places*
b   – Yogesh Chadha
    – Pamela Jooste
c   – 20th-century India
    – South Africa, during apartheid
d   – Mahatma Gandhi
    – a brother and sister
e   – Biography of Gandhi: he becomes a lawyer in Britain and South Africa and then goes back to India to lead the fight for independence.
    – The brother becomes part of the apartheid system, while the sister rebels against it. The book talks about what the brother learns from his experiences.
f   – Yes, because it is easy to understand and Gandhi is an interesting person of courage and integrity.
    – Yes, because it is well written and keeps you very interested.

C 2
a   *Bel Canto* is a book by Ann Patchett about love in a terrorist siege.
b   It starts off with a birthday party for Mr Hosokawa, a Japanese businessman.
c   It is set in the house of the vice-president in an unnamed Latin American country.
d   It tells a story of music and love in the middle of a terrorist kidnapping.
e   It is fantastically written.
f   It is un-put-downable

C 3
Possible answer
Bel Canto is a book by Ann Patchett about love and music in the middle of a terrorist kidnapping. It starts off with a party for Mr Hosokawa, a Japanese businessman, who loves opera. Rosanna Cox is an international opera star and she is flown in to sing. Terrorists arrive at the party and take the guests hostage. In this situation, two couples fall improbably in love and the story ends with both death and hope. I would definitely recommend this book as it has fantastic writing and it is un-put-downable. It has the perfect combination of music, love and fear.

UNIT 13
A 1
Finders keepers?
a   Philadelphia, 1981
b   Joey Coyle, 28, unemployed
c   more than $1million
d   He found it in a box in the street.
e   Yes.
f   He invested it foolishly and he lost it.
g   He was arrested, put in jail, then released; he died when they were making a movie of his story.

Man 1 Bank 0
a   San Francisco, 1995
b   Patrick Combs, 28, writer and speaker
c $95,093.35
d   He was sent a cheque.
e   No.

f   He gave it back.
g   He became a celebrity and a well-known motivational speaker.

A 2
a   5
b   6
c   4
d   9
e   1
f   7
g   3
h   2
i   8

A 3
a   9
b   7
c   2
d   5
e   1, 6, 10
f   3
g   8
h   4

A 4
a   with her pulse quickening
b   beyond his wildest dreams
c   nothing went right for him
d   luck was about to change
e   swore her to secrecy
f   putting people in touch with
g   make the most
h   made a mess of
i   to make matters worse
j   nothing to lose

B 1
a   a TV quiz show
b   the host / question master of *Who wants to be a millionaire?*
c   a contestant on *Who wants to be a millionaire?* who won a million pounds by cheating
d   the man who helped Charles Ingram by coughing

B 2
a   *Who wants to be a millionaire?*
b   the big prize for *Who wants to be a millionaire?*
c   an Anthony Eden
d   the question about the Anthony Eden
e   Charles Ingram
f   Tecwen Whittock
g   many in the audience
h   Diana Ingram, Charles' wife
i   a man sitting next to Tecwen Whittock
j   Charles, Diana and Tecwen
k   tapes from the show
l   Charles and Diana Ingram
m   Tecwen Whittock

B 3
a   host
b   contestant
c   increases
d   extract
e   garment
f   regular
g   on purpose
h   obvious
i   court
j   appropriate
k   administering
l   cheating

C 3
Possible answer
Name of writer: Juan Manuel Alvarez

Yes	More or less	No, not really
a	X	
b		X

c   1   he included more information about the people and more details about the story. What are the names of the people? What are they like? How long was the boy missing? Why did the father take the boy?
    2   he structured the writing better by using more paragraphs and if he corrected his mistakes.

C 4
a   I want to tell you
b   This crime happened
c   A little boy was kidnapped
d   People were sure
e   who took the boy
f   the father got mad
g   he couldn't have done it
h   suddenly
i   where he went
j   the police looked for the man
k   He was trying to leave
l   the father went to jail

UNIT 14

A 2
a   wide
b   burnt
c   The house appears to be sleeping in the summer heat – though it could also suggest that everyone in the house is sleeping through the heat of the day.
d   half-sleeping
e   go beyond, escape from
f   sheltering
g   yearning / wanting
h   kind of banana
i   reminder of home
j   moving from side to side
k   light
l   packed with letters
m   make-up for the lips
n   make-up for the face
o   not crisp anymore, and a little damaged, especially at the corners
p   smell
q   the essence of being a woman
r   grief

A 3
Possible answers
Similarities:
a   looking back on the past (all)
b   the Caribbean (*Midsummer, Tobago*; *Like a Beacon*)
c   memories of the poet's mother (*Like a Beacon*; *Handbag*)
Differences:
a   tropical heat (*Midsummer, Tobago*)
b   cold city a long way from home (*Like a Beacon*)
c   war remembered; smells (*Handbag*)

B 1
West Indian folk tales originally come from West Africa. They were changed in the West Indies by the addition of new animals.

B 2
The correct paragraph order is **k, i, g, f, b, j, d, h, a, e, c.**

B 3
a   Because Dog has sworn to break the bones of the thief who stole his pears (and that was Finger Quashy).
b   Because Dog's son had been playing with fire.
c   Because Dog came into the room with a big stick.
d   Because Rat told him that Finger Quashy had stolen some pears.
e   Because she wanted Dog to think that she was innocent.
f   Because Rat told him that she had.
g   Because everyone knew Dog was a good cook and made nice meals.
h   Because Dog blames them for the fire in his house – and for the fact that he hasn't got any clothes to wear any more.
i   Because she was so fast.
j   Because they were the best avocado pears for miles.

B 4
a   on fire
b   reduced to ashes
c   pantry
d   dignified
e   leapt
f   reprehensible
g   distracting
h   swearing
i   blamed
j   shot
k   it's not a bit like you
l   at his wits' end
m   yelling his head off
n   beside himself with fury

C 1
The correct order for the storyboards is **b, f, e, a, c, d.**

C 2
a   Exterior. Night. Ten years ago. A small side street in a city. Pools of light from street lights. Interior. The same night. A smoky café. Crowded. Edgy. ('Which opens': there is a verb, but the sentence is incomplete.)
b   exterior
c   pools of light
d   figure
e   crowded
f   furtively
g   edgy
h   pans
i   silhouetted

C 3
Possible answer
Scene 1: Exterior. Aerial shot of a beach. White sand. Glittering surf. Palm trees. The camera descends and pans along the beach. Bright sunlight. A young man runs towards us. He wears white T-shirt, blue shorts. No shoes.

Scene 2: Exterior. As before. The jogger runs past and away from us. Heavy breathing. He turns back to the camera as if afraid. He trips and pitches forward onto the sand.